C000264717

GREEN SHADOWS: A GURKHA STORY

GREEN SHADOWS: A GURKHA STORY

Denis Sheil-Small, MC

Foreword by
General Sir Walter Walker
KCB, CBE, DSO

WILLIAM KIMBER · LONDON

First published in 1982 by
WILLIAM KIMBER & CO. LIMITED
Godolphin House, 22a Queen Anne's Gate,
London SW1H 9AE

© Denis Sheil-Small, 1982

ISBN 0 7183 0129 3

This book is copyright. No part of it may be reproduced in any form without permission in writing from the publishers except by a reviewer who wishes to quote brief passages in connection with a review written for inclusion in a newspaper, magazine, radio or television broadcast

Photoset in North Wales by
Derek Doyle & Associates, Mold Clwyd,
and printed in Great Britain by
Garden City Press Limited,
Pixmore Avenue, Letchworth, Herts.

Contents

List of Illustrations

List of Maps in the Text

To all ranks of the 8th Gurkha Rifles who fell
in action during the Second World War.

Acknowledgements

Although *Green Shadows* is a personal account of the Burma Campaign I am indebted to the following sources for material used to check the accuracy of dates, places and units involved:

The Campaign in Burma (Frank Owen) published by Arrow Books (Proprietors: Hutchinson Ltd) in 1957. This is a new edition of the official account of *The Campaign in Burma* prepared by the Central Office of Information for South-East Asia Command, first published by HM Stationery Office in 1946. I quote from this work by kind permission of the Controller of HM Stationery Office and Messrs Hutchinson Ltd.

A Child in Arms (Patrick Davis) – Hutchinson & Co Ltd, 1970, for details of Pat Davis's patrolling activities when serving as my company officer.

History of the 8th Gurkha Rifles 1824-1949 (Lt-Col H.J. Huxford OBE) – Gale & Polden, 1952. Details of the Battle of Nyaungkashe were gleaned from this regimental history.

Some of the photographs reproduced in this book have been in my possession since 1942-1945 and were given to me by various brother officers. It is impossible to remember who donated what but I would like to thank them all the same. I am grateful to the Imperial War Museum for permission to reproduce other photographs kindly supplied by them.

Foreword

by

General Sir Walter Walker, KCB, CBE, DSO

It has been said that every one of us has the makings of at least one book locked up inside us. If this old saying be true, then this is certainly applicable to Major Denis Sheil-Small, MC and his book *Green Shadows*.

Already well-known in military circles as co-author of *The Gurkhas, The Undeclared War* and *A Pride of Gurkhas*, Denis Sheil-Small has now written this most moving story of his personal experiences in Burma during World War II, culminating in the award of the Victoria Cross to Rifleman Lachhiman Gurung of the 4/8th Gurkha Rifles.

I commanded this battalion as a lieutenant-colonel at the time of the battles described in this book and the events so vividly and accurately described by the author evoke memories of the smoke and flame of battle so familiar to all who have passed through this experience.

The battle in which the author endured his first baptism of fire, won his spurs as a company commander and gained the award of the Military Cross, was the first pitched battle to which the battalion had been committed after all the intensive retraining carried out at Kohima. Denis Sheil-Small and his company of Gurkha infantrymen took the full impact of this traumatic and psychologically important battle. They acquitted themselves with honour.

In recommending this young officer for the Immediate Award of the Military Cross I had this to say in the Citation:

At Ywathit, on the east bank of the Irrawaddy, on the morning of the 5th March 1945, Major Sheil-Small, a company commander, was reconnoitring a vital feature which was to be occupied by his company, when the enemy launched an attack in great strength.

This officer's company had only just taken up its dispositions and were about to dig in. The feature consisted of barren, stony, knife-edge ridges with no cover whatsoever. The enemy, who outnumbered the company by more than 3 to 1, put down an intense concentration of artillery, mortar, grenade discharger, medium and light machine gun and small arms fire, which swept the ridges and pinned this company to the ground. Behind this concentration the enemy made a frontal assault which was smashed up. The enemy then encircled the position, and attempted to assault from the flanks and rear. In spite of the withering fire, and although no man had any cover whatsoever, everyone held his ground, and the enemy was met by fierce and accurate fire from rifles, light automatics and grenades. Major Sheil-Small, by his utter disregard for his own safety, by the cool manner in which he conducted this magnificent stand, by his refusal to give up one inch to the enemy, so inspired his men that they not only smashed up every assault, but counter-attacked down the barren slopes. The enemy was so shaken that he retired in confusion leaving 39 dead and carrying away with him a great number of wounded. While he was retreating he was pounded with artillery and machine gun fire and many more casualties were inflicted on him.

I consider it is most important that the present and future generations of younger officers should be made aware of the smell of battle and of how one young officer – a citizen soldier and not a Regular officer at that – stood up to his first shock of battle.

The story unfolded in this book affords the reader a glimpse of the truly outstanding qualities and personal bravery of this magnificent race of Gurkhas who still render inestimable service to the British Crown as part of the modern British Army. It also provides an insight into the reserves of strength and endurance which lie fallow within us all, awaiting only our own personal trial.

This book should provide compulsive reading for all who still revere the badge of courage.

Salisbury,
18 December 1981

WALTER WALKER

The Yellow Tide

The tiny village had no name; at least, there was nothing to indicate it marked on my map.

A few bamboo huts, raised high on stilts and thatched with palm leaves, clustered together in a small clearing. All about them rose the massive teak trees of the jungle in Burma, just across the border from Assam, near Tamu. Not a single human being was in sight.

The largest hut was encircled by a compound of dried mud; I decided to investigate this place before searching the other dwellings. On my signal, the Gurkha riflemen comprising my patrol moved up from behind me, halted and silently took up their positions commanding the approaches to the hut.

As I crossed the compound, I saw a complete skeleton stretched out on the ground, clothed in the tattered remnants of a Japanese uniform. The feet were encased in shrivelled and cracked leather army boots which fell apart at a touch. The skull had parted from the neck and lay a little to one side, the jaw bones locked open with the large prominent teeth set in the senseless grin of death.

It seemed clear to me that this soldier had been crawling in search of water when he finally collapsed, for under his outstretched hand lay an empty water bottle.

Passing on from this gruesome sight, I entered the house. There, as my eyes accustomed themselves to the gloom after the dazzling sunlight outside, I saw a bamboo sleeping platform on the top of which lay six more skeletons clad in scanty and tattered loincloths. An empty water bottle lay beside each of the skeletons.

One could visualise their hopeless and bitter end; the retreat down from the Imphal Plain, that killing ground of the Japanese army, our troops harassing and pressing at their heels, our Air Force hammering them from above and out of the blinding sun. Their line of supply had virtually ceased to exist and they were forced to live off the land. No doubt their unit had entered this village to find that the Burmese had fled, taking with them all food supplies. Desperately wounded, or stricken by fever, these six men and the lone seventh outside had been left behind as the others pushed on, their only solace – a water bottle from which to slake their thirst.

Too weak to move, they had lasted a day or two until the water gave out. Then the strongest had crawled across the floor and out into the glare of the sun, clasping his water bottle and searching in anguish for a well. Either the sun, or the effects of his wounds, finished him for he never returned to his comrades. One by one they also succumbed, until all had perished at the end of their long and bloody road from Japan.

I looked down at the sight and felt moved to pity. Across my mind, however, came the memory of British, Australian, Indian and Gurkha troops who had fallen alive into the hands of these same Japanese; men crucified, beheaded, used as living dummies for the horror of bayonet practice or subjected to other unspeakable tortures.

The pity died within me and, turning on my heels, I went out to rejoin my Gurkhas.

This was 1945 and the tide of war was turning. The Imperial Japanese Army, after losing 65,000 men in the bloody fighting around Imphal and Kohima, had fallen back on the defensive across the Burma border and was retreating. By May of that year it had been hurled back across the Irrawaddy River, was withdrawing from Mandalay and was extricating the remaining hard core of the army from the Arakan. The situation thus conjured up at last thoughts of final victory for the troops of the Fourteenth Army. But it had not always been thus.

The war correspondents attached to our forces had long been starved of success stories during their stay with us. Their despatches had, of necessity, to treat of the eternal and heart-rending fight of those troops against the jungle, the mountains, the swamps, the heat, thirst, fevers – a fight of ordinary, simple men, sustained only by their personal courage and faith against a ruthless, cruel and fanatical enemy. The incredible Japanese military machine had carried them forward on the wave of success until the yellow tide had lapped the very shores and boundaries of India.

Now, however, their despatches took on a new colour. The Japanese communications had begun to collapse; the enemy was short of food, ammunition, medical supplies; his air support had almost vanished. All these factors seemed to point to only one result – an end to the campaign.

The campaigner, however, knows from bitter experience that no battle ends until the last shot has been fired. Indeed, through this knowledge, many a victory has been snatched in the face of tremendous odds.

Above all, the men of our Forgotten Army, who now found the reluctant spotlight of publicity focussed upon them, after so long in their dark green shadows, did not underestimate the Japanese. It is not surprising, therefore, that some of the most vicious, bloody and bitter fighting was yet to come, whilst the Powers-that-be were busily preparing plans for the Victory Parade to be held in Rangoon.

The Japanese fought to the last gasp wherever we found them; they died singly, in fives, in tens and in hundreds with a fanaticism that was awe-inspiring. From the north-west corner of Burma, down through all that ravished land, we pursued them to the south-east exit across the Sittang River to Siam. In holes and corners, in jungle and plain they turned, snarling, to hit back savagely and to inflict mounting casualties amongst us.

It was one of these engagements that brought to the 4/8th Gurkha Rifles the distinction of the only Victoria Cross awarded to this regiment during the Second World War.

The Victoria Cross was, of course, awarded to several Gurkhas who belonged to other Gurkha regiments but in the case of our own regiment this ultimate award for outstanding bravery was won by Rifleman Lachhiman Gurung, who twelve months previously had arrived in our training centre in India as a shy young recruit.

I had the honour to train, serve with and command this splendid Gurkha soldier and the following story relates my experiences with the battalion from the time of leaving our training centre until the last desperate battle which gained for Rifleman Lachhiman an outstanding place in military history.

CHAPTER ONE

The Road to War

The fame of the Gurkhas has spread across the world and wherever fighting men have gathered together there is not one who has ever failed to salute their name.

From the days of the last century, through the Indian Mutiny, the Naga Wars, the early Burma Wars and even the Tibetan Campaign of 1903/4 these magnificent soldiers have proved themselves to be loyal and courageous fighters. During the First World War thousands of Allied soldiers in France and Flanders, Mesopotamia, Gallipoli, Egypt and Palestine became familiar with the large Gurkha felt hat worn slanting across the head of the Gurkha rifleman, and marvelled at his stamina and endurance, perfected by training in the Khyber Pass and amongst the arid hills of the North-West Frontier of India.

With the advent of the Second World War, the little mountain kingdom of Nepal was destined to contribute to the Allied cause a greater number of soldiers, in proportion to her population, than any other country. There were ten regiments of Gurkhas, comprising the old Gurkha Brigade, and in this war each regiment raised and despatched no less than four battalions on active service. In North Africa, Italy, Iraq, Burma, Assam and Java they continued to enhance their reputation, to strike fear into their enemies and to gain respect and affection from those who fought alongside them. In the years which followed that war Gurkha regiments forming part of the British Army gained further laurels in Malaya and Borneo where they proved themselves to be masters of the jungle.

These stocky, slant-eyed children of Nepal are by tradition soldiers, volunteers all, who take an intense pride in their calling. Their home environment on the slopes of the Himalayas produces sturdy bodies powered by hearts that will endure to the end. Their nature is simple, straightforward and loyal, enriched with a sense of humour that is an asset to any fighting man. It was indeed a privilege to serve with them.

It was whilst I was a cadet at the Officers' Training School at Bangalore, in Southern India, that I first set eyes on Gurkha troops. A demonstration platoon arrived on the scene to illustrate for us a lesson in mountain warfare. The turn-out, smartness of drill and the efficiency of these cheerful little men confirmed all the stories which I had heard about them. I was glad that I had already made my choice to join their regiment when granted my commission.

In due course I found myself reporting to the Regimental Training Centre of the 8th Gurkha Rifles at Quetta, truly a far-flung military outpost of the British Empire. Amongst those arid, treeless hills at the western end of the North-West Frontier of India and on those stony, barren parade grounds I was to absorb in full the language, customs and spirit of this charming race of people until, with pride, I identified myself completely with them.

Month after month passed by and the snows up there came and went. It was with a feeling of achievement that we would see our young recruits change from shy boys into seasoned riflemen, expert with their weapons and trained in all the complexities of modern warfare.

Our task was simplified by the Gurkha Officers. Holders of the Viceroy's commission, these veterans formed the connecting link between the NCOs and the British officers and their influence was profound. Each one had fifteen or more years of service behind him and had been tested in action on the Frontier.

Straight as ramrods, chests ablaze with campaign medal ribbons, their bush shirts and shorts starched in knife-edge creases, they commanded respect wherever they appeared. The discipline in a Gurkha regiment was severe, perhaps extreme. It is not by chance that the Gurkhas have won such distinction in battle. Courage without discipline is not enough. These Gurkha officers applied themselves ceaselessly to instil into those recruits obedience to orders which welded them together as a unit.

It was not only the recruits who benefited from the experience of these fine men. I well remember my first day as a new subaltern on the parade ground. My knowledge of the Gurkhali language was nil and my Urdu (or Hindustani) was quite elementary, being limited

to certain phrases from the textbook which we all had studied for
the examination as cadets. Fortunately, the words of command for
drill purposes were in English, so I was able to start the parade off
without a catastrophe, but the thought of conducting an intelligent
conversation in this foreign tongue with these eager, smart soldiers
caused beads of perspiration to burst out on my forehead in spite of
the early morning chill.

Taking the bull by the horns, I turned to the Subadar, who was
the senior Gurkha officer present, and delivered some atrocious
platitude in my halting Urdu. Springing to attention, he favoured
me with an impeccable salute and returned the compliment, whilst
a dazzling smile spread across his brown face. In the conversation
which followed, he gently corrected my vocabulary and grammar,
at the same time putting me completely at my ease. After a day or
two he started to repeat my Urdu sentences in Gurkhali and thus I
made my first acquaintance with that intriguing language.

The fascination of it all gripped me from the outset. My contact
was, on the one hand, with these splendid veterans, and, on the
other, with the newly arrived recruits from Nepal who reached
Quetta after the very first train journey of their lives. Until then
many of them had never seen a train, motor car, clock, or worn a
pair of boots. Each one of them had to become a fully trained
soldier by the end of seven months. It seemed impossible, but the
impossible was achieved.

The lorry droned steadily onward and upward and I swayed gently
backwards and forwards with the motion of the vehicle.

With several companions, I was moving up the Kohima Road
from the railhead on the last leg of the journey to join my battalion
– the 4/8th Gurkha Rifles. The days in the training centre were over
and all that they had taught me there was to be put to the test. The
other occupants of the lorry were fellow-travellers from various
regiments who, like myself, had left the transit camp at Dimapur
that morning. Like myself, they were reinforcements and, like
myself, they sat silently in the jolting vehicle, each totally occupied
with his private thoughts. Our eyes were sharp to note the evidence
of war as our lorry ate up mile after mile of the steep and tortuous
road.

The scenery was magnificent. Assam is a country of exquisite hills and mountains, on the slopes of which lie the beautiful Tea Gardens for which the land is renowned. Dimapur, the village which now lay behind us, was the railhead for the Fourteenth Army on this front. It consisted of a collection of bamboo bashas and a bazaar which formed the original settlement in peace-time. Now, it had grown into a straggling Army base including a hospital, rest camps for British and Indian troops, together with various important dumps belonging to the ancillary forces whose task was to keep the guns firing and the troops clothed and fed.

The railway station at Dimapur was the end of the line. Men who detrained there had reached the end of journeys from the four corners of India, from East Africa, West Africa and from England herself. There were no platforms; you just climbed down onto the track and knew that you had arrived.

We were not sorry to leave Dimapur after our enforced stay there. The place lies in a depression and at that particular time of the year the heat was terrific. The humidity added to the discomfort. One did not merely perspire there; the sweat burst through your pores with positive violence, drenching your battledress and turning the colour of your clothing from jungle green to black.

At night, instead of the cool breezes of the mountains, the heat continued unabated and seemed to be intensified by the darkness. Troops were under canvas in the transit camp and the tents served only to suffocate you in that enervating atmosphere.

Up and up went the lorry. As we climbed higher and higher, the air gradually grew crisp and tangy with unmistakeable mountain freshness. The road curved and twisted around hairpin bends reputed to be the most treacherous in the world. On one side the ground fell away straight down into valleys hundreds of feet below; on the other it rose cliff-like until it was lost in jungle-clad peaks high above us. At one point our shuddering lorry stopped by a lone figure sitting disconsolately by the roadside. The Indian sepoy rose to his feet and pointed down into the gorge. On being questioned he revealed that he was the driver of an Indian Army Service Corps lorry that had slid over the edge of the precipice and now lay smashed to pieces some two hundred feet below, with its contents strewn around it. Fortunately, he was the only occupant and had saved himself by throwing himself out of his driving seat as the nearside wheels went over the edge.

With our new, shocked, passenger aboard we ground slowly on, passing various staging posts, dumps of food and ammunition, workshops and, more and more frequently, we caught sight of the Red Cross flag fluttering above the tents of the Advanced Dressing Stations and First Aid Posts.

There could be little doubt that we were close to the Front. The activity increased as we journeyed on, the road ahead of us appearing to hurry into the embrace of the mountains around us. By mid-day our complaining vehicle whined up the last incline and we had reached Kohima, whose name was already well-known to all of us. It was here that the much vaunted and publicised Japanese invasion of India was finally halted and turned amidst terrible privation and carnage.

We were at the summit of a mountain ridge, 5,000 feet up, in a saddle joining two higher mountain peaks. Our questing eyes saw everywhere the evidence of bitter battle. On all sides the trees were stripped clean of foliage and branches; the ground was scarred with foxholes or trenches and gashed by shellholes. To our right rose the shattered bulk of Jail Hill, linked to the other features whose names had already become bywords – GPT Ridge and DIS Hill; to the left, the road wound along through the native village to the heights beyond.

Here we lost some of our passengers and the remainder of us moved on over the crest and started down the long winding road towards Imphal.

At Milestone 109 I had reached my own destination and I climbed stiffly down over the tailboard of the lorry. Looking around at the jungle at the side of the road, I spotted the figure of a Gurkha amongst some trees and he led me to the officer in charge. As I entered a bamboo basha, well concealed off the road, I saw two figures in the gloom. One I recognised as Brian Irving – a young officer whom I had last seen in the training centre, back in India; the other was an older man who was introduced to me as Ted Kemp. He was a man I came to know and like very well.

To my disappointment, I discovered that only the sick and wounded men of the battalion were here. After flying from their battles in the Arakan into the relief of Imphal, the remainder of the battalion had routed the Japanese out of their mountain base at Ukhrul and was now pounding them into the hills. Ted Kemp pointed to a steep jungle-covered hill across the road.

'They went over that three days ago and will not be back for some time,' he said. 'For the time being you had better remain here'.

At his invitation I dumped my kit in a corner and joined them both in their evening meal.

Quetta seemed to be very far away as a smiling Gurkha rifleman produced two mess tins heaped high with rice and curried meat, and held out his hand for mine. It was soon filled and replaced before me and I discovered that I was famished after the long journey. Following the food came steaming mugs of strong, sweet tea.

As we talked, I took stock of my two companions. Both were clearly sick men; their faces showing signs of great strain on the haggard features. This was not surprising after the ordeal which they had undergone in the Arakan and in the operations around Imphal after the Dakota aircraft had disgorged them on the landing strip at Imphal. I was to notice later how thin and haggard the men also looked, their ribs showing plainly in many cases after a year of continuous jungle warfare.

I heard of the Arakan fighting, the Battle of the Admin Box, and of the airlift to Imphal of the whole of the 7th Indian Division, to which we belonged. It was a stirring tale of hardship and battle and bold strategy on the grand scale. It was clear to me that my life from now on would be far from dull in such company.

During the evening our conversation was interrupted by the ringing of the field telephone that stood on a table in the corner of the basha. After a short talk with someone at the other end of the wire, Ted Kemp replaced the receiver and turned to me with an apology.

'I don't quite know what this is all about,' he said, 'but you have to return to Dimapur to-morrow morning. They want a liaison officer for this brigade and he must be able to speak Gurkhali.'

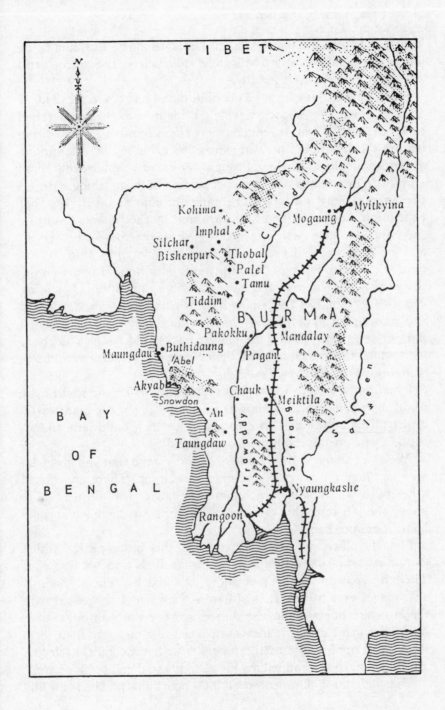

Next day I entered the rest camp at Dimapur after a long and tiring journey back down from Milestone 109 where Ted Kemp, still apologising, had waved goodbye.

Since leaving this camp the previous day, I had covered 218 miles up and down the road over which Wingate's men had marched early in 1942 when setting out on their hazardous expedition behind the Japanese lines, an expedition criticised by the pundits as being suicidal and which brought fame to a few, hardship to all and death or wounds to a large proportion of those taking part. Of the three young officers from our Gurkha regiment on that expedition, one was killed, one captured by the Japanese and the surviving youngster was awarded the Military Cross for bravery in action. They were all personal friends of mine and I studied that road with mixed feelings. Within twenty-four hours I had seen the devastation at Kohima and the incredible difficulties of fighting over this terrain, but I was now back where I had started, the war was moving ahead of me and somehow for the moment I felt flat. It did not seem right that I, the newcomer, should be back safely at base whilst the others, after all their bitter experiences, should still be fighting for their lives.

I made my way to the Camp Adjutant's office situated in the usual bamboo basha amongst the trees. The occupant, who returned my salute and rose to his feet, was a handsome Indian captain who introduced himself as Achmed.

'Welcome to our camp,' he said. 'I understand that you are to be attached here for a week or so on a special job. There are several other officers from different regiments and we will all hear more about the job later this afternoon. There is a conference at 1600 hours. See you then.'

I left the office and was directed to another basha nearby which contained four string charpoys or Indian beds and nothing else. Though spartan in appearance, the basha offers distinct advantages over a tent. It is of bamboo construction, roofed with thatch which offers shade, the slatted walls permit ventilation and, in a permanent camp, it may even boast of a concrete floor. Still thinking of my friends at Milestone 109 with some guilt, I selected an empty charpoy, dumped my kit upon it and then lit a cigarette.

The conference commenced at 1600 hours sharp. The presiding

officer was a dark, saturnine major from a British regiment – the Northamptonshire Regiment. Seated around a table there were three British and four Indian officers. They all wore divisional flashes on the shoulders of their green battledresses and had quite clearly just come down from the forward areas.

The major began.

'My name's Britton; we're here to organize and despatch leave parties to India. Leave has been a luxury which none of us has been able to afford during this bloody campaign. The Japanese have been defeated for the first time at Kohima and Imphal and before we press on to finish the job and destroy their army the powers-that-be have decreed that we refresh ourselves for the task ahead. Only Indian and Gurkha troops will pass through this camp.'

He looked around and smiled.

'With typical army humour they have selected four of us from British regiments and we do not speak the language. We will need a lot of help from you gentlemen.'

I looked across at the Indian officers who saw the joke and laughed, but I did not feel quite so comfortable. I was the only Gurkhali-speaking officer present and my talents as a linguist were going to receive a severe test.

We took note of all the arrangements and then broke up.

My companions introduced themselves – Wilfred, also from the Northants, Ted Moore from the Queen's and Val Adams from the Devons. The Indian officers were from the Punjab Regiment, the Jats, the Sikhs, and the Rajputana Rifles.

That evening the troops started to arrive, first in small batches, then in larger numbers and, later, over the next few weeks, in a positive flood. In they came to the camp, straight from their recent ordeal and I was struck at once by their cheerfulness and their military bearing. One could not doubt that this was a victorious army. From Imphal, Kohima, Ukhrul, Bishenpur, Palel, Tiddim, they came; places destined to figure on the battle honours and standards of regiments throughout the British and Indian Armies. From Kennedy Peak, Fort White, the Chocolate Staircase and from scores of nameless mountain ridges. Every division and every military unit passed its men through the camp on their first and only leave for over a year.

The Japanese have since admitted that in the Kohima-Imphal battle area alone 65,000 perished – here were the men who had destroyed them. I felt an overwhelming sense of pride as I regarded them.

On the second day I spotted the badges of my own regiment amongst the arrivals and I hastened forward to give them a special welcome. I was warmed by their cheerful smiles and heartened by their tales of success. It was a great day.

We soon slipped into an efficient routine. Each day the men who had sheltered overnight were refreshed, fed, paid by the field cashier and entrained on their long journeys. Leave in the Indian Army was not a matter of hours or days. It required at least a month to ensure that a soldier should reach his village, spend a week or so there and make the return journey. Gurkha troops, after a long and arduous railway trip, may have over a week on foot in front of them before reaching their families living on the mountain slopes of the Himalayas in Nepal. Rivers have to be crossed by perilous, swinging wooden bridges which are swept away each year in the rainy season as the melting snows from 20,000 feet mountain peaks turn them into swirling, rushing torrents.

After our day's work was completed, we would sit outside the basha in a clearing surrounded by massive trees that rose straight up into the black night, their tops invisible. During these evenings we got to know each other very well. There was a tannoy loudspeaker system fitted up amongst the trees and someone found an old gramophone and some records. The result was an evening concert, repeated each night, of old and popular tunes. It was with a musical background of the Ink Spots singing 'Every Night About This Time' that I heard first hand accounts of the bitter fighting at Kohima and the dreadful frontal attacks on Jail Hill, Church Knoll and other strongly-held Japanese positions; places now littered with the graves of British, Indian and Gurkha troops and pervaded by the sickly-sweet stench of death from the rotting Japanese corpses lying in unknown parts of the jungle where they had fallen.

In such surroundings and under such circumstances the thought of romance was very far from my mind. Strange, however, are the influences which shape our lives at all times.

Farther down the road from the camp there was a large base

hospital and helping to staff it were some nursing sisters of the Queen Alexandra's Imperial Nursing Service. Their own hospital at Kohima had been overrun by the Japanese and these girls had been evacuated to Dimapur. They had no home of their own and lived in our rest camp when off duty from the hospital.

We saw little of these sisters as their hours of duty were onerous and long, but at mealtime they would appear in the mess basha, sit at their own table, eat their own soya link bread and sausages like the rest of us and then disappear. At night they would come off duty at 2000 hours and after their supper they would vanish in the direction of their bashas, each with a hurricane lamp to guide them, like so many fireflies amongst the trees.

The sight of these ladies and their aura of femininity entranced us. Many a longing glance was cast in their direction but they appeared to be truly untouchable as they glided in and out of the mess, always under the eagle eye of their dignified and formidable matron.

One evening, Major Britton remarked that this segregation of the sexes seemed to him to be unfriendly and he thought that we also must regret it.

'We must break the ice,' he said – an apt simile for that sweltering place.

After a discussion it was agreed that we should invite the matron to join us in a nightcap that evening and it was with great interest that we awaited the approach of the evening meal. After supper Matron was duly button-holed and, to our satisfaction, accepted our invitation. On acquaintance she proved to be a woman of great charm and when it was tentatively suggested that we might all take our meals together, instead of being separated, she accepted the idea without hesitation.

The following evening one or two of the sisters were introduced to us and from that time on the meals became rather more interesting. The monotony of the food appeared less obvious as we all chatted and picked the weevils out of our bread. At the end of the week, after a little pressure from us, the tables and chairs were cleared out of the basha and we enjoyed an impromptu dance, although the same tunes were repeated at regular intervals as the old gramophone rendered loyal service in the corner.

It was shortly after this that I met my future wife.

I was invited to the sergeants' mess basha by a sergeant in the Devons who worked with me on the leave details during the daytime. I accepted with great pleasure and when I arrived I found that there was a party in progress to celebrate someone's birthday. Some of the sisters had also accepted invitations and our friend the old gramophone had been borrowed for the occasion.

Sally was sitting with another sister, chatting to the Camp Commandant. She was petite, dark and looked most attractive. After we had been introduced, we drifted apart and I spent most of the evening chatting to the sergeant who was a typical Devon countryman, with a delightful burr in his voice.

Several days later, Sally accompanied the matron to one of our evening 'night-caps', and we met again. It was from her that I first heard details of 'The Flap', which was the local term for the events leading up to the battle at Kohima and the consternation at Dimapur when a Japanese patrol appeared a few miles away from the base itself. She also told me with sadness of a very charming, gentle Indian doctor in her hospital who had stayed behind to serve the wounded when the remainder of the staff were ordered out. He was the surgeon; but died later after his own leg was blown off.

To my mind, Sally was typical of all those sisters who, in those shockingly primitive conditions, carried out their duties with such great cheerfulness and efficiency. Thousands of sick and wounded had cause to remember them with gratitude. They succoured the living and comforted the dying.

At the end of several more weeks the last train had left Dimapur, crowded with its eager leave party, and our job was finished.

Together we drank our last nightcap and said goodbye next morning with more than a tinge of regret. I only hope that they all survived the hardships and the fighting which followed. Val Adams I met again in Quetta when I returned from Burma; of the others I have never heard any news.

CHAPTER TWO

Kohima Interlude

It was December, but our preparations were certainly not for Christmas. Instead, for several months the battalion had undergone intensive training for the big advance into Burma.

After my stint of duty at Dimapur, I had finally caught up with the 4/8th Gurkha Rifles where they had pitched tents on a mountain spur some miles east of the shattered village of Kohima. By now the war had rumbled south, where the Japs had retired across the Chindwin River and were preparing to withdraw across the Irrawaddy, one of the greatest rivers in the world. We knew that soon we must be called upon once again to play our part and we were determined that we should not be unprepared.

Every day we practised weapon training, bayonet fighting, shooting and marching; but above all we studied the Japanese method of warfare. We climbed every mountain peak around Kohima; we probed into every Jap foxhole; we saw how they sited their positions; we sat in them and studied the actual ground in crossing which so many of our own troops had recently died. We learned of the reverse slope position where the concealed machine gun annihilates the victors as they pause to consolidate the position already won. We thought of the Japanese, we talked of the Japanese and from them we learned our lesson for the future.

Then came the digging.

We dug on the slopes of hills, on the tops of ridges and on the flat. We dug by day and at night we sat in the foxholes we had dug, whilst our own troops attacked us under cover of live ammunition fired over our heads. Companies were sent to attack each other by day and by night and all the time patrols were out, perfecting their technique.

To those veterans who had been in action before this was merely a continuation of their war experience, but to me and to other reinforcements it was invaluable. I am firmly convinced that the success of our patrols later achieved in Burma was due to the activities of that December.

I wandered alone into the Naga Village above Kohima.

A little boy came out from the ruins of a hut, a bowl of food in his hand, and sat down to eat his evening meal. The smell of wood smoke was in the air as the Nagas busied themselves about their cooking. All around was dirt and drabness. Pigs rooted amongst the bare, grey stones and here and there a half-starved dog yelped at my approach.

I became aware of a figure at my side and as I turned a voice said, 'Good evening, Sir.'

I beheld a Naga, dressed not in the traditional red blanket affected by these head hunters but in shirt and shorts. He was one of the few English-speaking Christian Nagas.

'May I help you, Sir?' he went on.

As I was looking for old Japanese positions I thanked him for his courtesy and indicated that I was just looking around.

The Naga attached himself to me and whilst we chatted I was shown the new tin roofs on the surrounding huts which had been shattered during the recent battle. 'Gift of Government,' the Naga said with pride.

I left him and moved on to continue my search. I found several positions and examined them with interest, together with the discarded flotsam of war which lay about: rusty and smashed Japanese and British helmets, ammunition boxes, broken bayonets, shell cases, punctured water bottles and pieces of Jap leather equipment baked hard by sun and wind. Suddenly a gleam caught my eye and I turned towards it.

A solid block of grey stone jutted up from the surrounding filth and squalor. There, on the stone, cut out in tin, was the figure of a Highlander, kilts a-swing and bagpipes skirling. The shimmer of the tin seemed to imbue him with life. This was the memorial to the Cameron Highlanders who stood and fell here in the battle for Kohima.

As the first tendrils of the evening mountain mist reached out from the surrounding peaks and the blue wood smoke eddied about the figure, my thoughts were transported to the purple-clad hills of the Highlands and I felt the silence pregnant about me. A chill crept through me and, shivering, I turned and left the Highlander alone amidst the haze and the swirling mists.

As the weeks passed by I settled into the life of the battalion and came to know the officers and men. In an Indian Army battalion there were only some twelve British officers and a feeling of unity and mutual respect was essential for morale. There was no place for the shirker and no place for any coterie of officers holding aloof on some imagined privilege of caste. We were like a large family and we had to fraternize.

We were commanded by Lieutenant-Colonel Walter Walker, who gained fame and promotion during the post-war years as General Sir Walter Walker, KCB, CBE, DSO, and who revealed even at this time those attributes and total dedication to duty that were to raise him to the pinnacle of his profession.

The Colonel and the second-in-command were both Regular officers and the remainder of us came from widely differing civilian callings. Amongst us we had a bank clerk, a textile salesman, an insurance official and also several young officers with whom the war had caught up before they had launched out on any career; they had come fresh from school into the ranks and had now become seasoned soldiers. We also had an American, Lieutenant Scott Gilmore, who had been a volunteer ambulance driver in the Middle East before Pearl Harbour, and who had joined the Indian Army when his country came into the struggle. He was a character indeed, whose pronunciation of Gurkhali in the New York twang astonished and delighted the Gurkhas themselves. He later proved himself in battle a man of stature. The bond that united us all was our affection for the Gurkhas.

I had been posted to 'C' Company which was commanded by Major Peter Myers. This officer had been with the battalion since their first taste of fighting in the Arakan and he had been awarded the Military Cross for the part he played in the recent battle at Ukhrul. He possessed a Gurkha hat with a neat hole drilled through the crown where a bullet had pierced the front of the hat and passed out through the back. As both holes were low on the crown and, in fact, through the pugaree, it was clear that the bullet must have parted Peter's thick black hair. I must admit that I regarded this hat with a certain amount of awe and as an omen of things to come.

It was a source of great satisfaction to me to be associated with Peter. I listened carefully to all that he had to impart and learned a good deal by observation. When he went off on leave later I pursued our training programme under the critical but kindly eyes of the Gurkha subadar and his fellow Gurkha officers in charge of the platoons. Little could I guess that one of these riflemen listening so carefully to my lectures was later to win the Victoria Cross.

Despite the fact that the battalion had been well and truly blooded in action, training continued week after week and intensified under the personal supervision of the Colonel, who had seen the disaster of the retreat out of Burma during the First Burma Campaign when he was GS01 to the 1st Burma Division. He was determined that we would not make mistakes in the forthcoming fighting. Walter Walker was a martinet; there is no doubt of that. He was also a perfectionist. If your foxholes or bunkers were not properly dug, you dug them again; spoil from digging was not left heaped around trenches, it was spirited away to the rear in sandbags so that those trenches would not be visible to the Japanese; if a practice attack faltered or became ragged under the blazing sun, then the sweating troops would be ordered back to the start line to attack again. Officers were far from immune. If your field orders were faulty or imprecise you were rocketed later with withering scorn. Even the latrines did not escape his eagle eye. They must not be less than six feet deep, properly sited and well looked after.

At times we became exasperated. Other units nearby did not seem to be going through the hoop as we were. The division was on rest and we thought that this was a peculiar way to 'rest'.

Later, we took part in brigade exercises and it was during a really large cheme that I discovered at first hand the rigours of patrolling through dense bamboo jungle on the slopes of a lofty mountain.

The exercise had already lasted for several days and nights and we found ourselves some twenty miles from Kohima, weary and

(Right) 8th Gurkha Rifles
Regimental Training Centre,
Quetta, 1943. The
Subadar-Major talks to a
Jemadar (Platoon Commander)

(Left) 8th Gurkha Rifles
Regimental Training Centre,
Quetta, 1943. Battalion
Havildar-Major and a Naik.

8th Gurkha Rifles, Quetta, 1943. The Khud (mountain) Race. Coming down (good practice for the North-West Frontier!).

(Left) March 1943. Desert Warfare Camp at Sibi (Sind Desert). Second-Lieutenant Quentin Kennedy, killed at Nyaungkashe, Burma, 1945. *(Right)* Sibi, 1943. Lieutenant Tony Brand Crombie.

jaded. We sat around the Colonel at the summit of a hill for the umpteenth set of orders. This time, to our intense relief, he announced that all was over. Smiles broke out on our faces and our thoughts turned eagerly to the comfort of our tents back at camp. I had a feeling that I could sleep undisturbed for twenty-four hours.

'One last task confronts us,' said the Colonel. 'The Brigadier wants a patrol to survey a route from here to that mountain over there.' He pointed to a peak rising out of the blue haze across a deep valley.

We all stiffened.

Slowly the Colonel's gaze travelled around our circle and across our taut faces. Finally, it came to rest upon me.

'Denis,' he said. 'You can tackle this one. Take a platoon and move off now. I want a good report. Find a route to the summit and ascertain whether it is jeepable, safe for mules or only good for troops on foot.'

I could see the relief on the other faces around me and hear their pent-up breath coming out in gasps at being passed over. I tried to look unconcerned but this was indeed a blow to my rosy visions of camp.

After the Colonel dismissed us, the leg-pulling began.

'See you next week.'

'Send us a telegram if you ever get there.'

'I'll have a beer for you when we get back to camp.'

'Look out for snakes.'

I joined ruefully in the laughter, shouldered my pack, slipped my arm through the sling of my sten gun, and moved away to collect the unfortunate platoon.

Our route lay straight down the mountain slope and the ground dropped alarmingly as we progressed. We moved in single file, the better to negotiate a path through the lush vegetation. After about 500 yards we came to dense bamboo jungle spreading across our front like the bars of a cage. There was no way around it.

I detailed two men as cutters at the head of the patrol and their kukris were soon swinging. The further we went, the denser it became, until soon our progress was down to a crawl. Fresh cutters took over from the two sweating Gurkhas but their task was tough. As the evening shadows lengthened I called a halt for the evening meal; shortly afterwards total darkness enveloped us.

With the coming of night the temperature fell swiftly and soon we were all shivering where we sat. Further progress was clearly out of the question and a very cold night lay ahead. I realized that, officially, we were still on exercise, in enemy country and that, for security, the lighting of fires should be out of the question. My soldierly instincts forbade a fire; but the old civilian lurking inside me felt quite bolshie at the thought of the rest of the battalion, by now doubtless back amongst the comforts of the camp. I thought of the past two days and their tiring marches up and down valleys and hills. I looked at the shivering Gurkhas and I gave the order to light a big fire. Even my two Gurkha officers, who should have scolded me, looked delighted. The men greeted the idea with great enthusiasm and down crashed some more bamboo ready for the blaze. The heat of burning bamboo is intense and cold was banished for the rest of the night.

With sunrise, we took some food and then pressed on, fortified by our rest. It was still tough going but as the day progressed we reached the bottom of the valley where a stream ran swiftly between rocks and boulders, flanked by jungle on either side. We waded through the water which was cold to our perspiring bodies. However, we found it quite impossible to make a way through the dense vegetation on the other side.

The only solution lay in passage along the bed of the stream, in hope of better things. We clambered for hours through the water and over the rocks, testing our endurance and twisting more than one ankle. At last we found a small gap in the green wall of jungle and thankfully left the water behind us. Steeply the ground rose and soon we were panting with our efforts at climbing. Bamboo seemed to be growing in plantations, alternating with dense undergrowth and we strove to cut straight through it.

By now it was late afternoon and we were already overdue at the rendezvous arranged by the battalion, which was a track on the top of the mountain. Progress was still slow and in due course the evening shadows again crept over us. Just before dark we reached a spot where a massive cliff rose straight in front of us, overhanging our patrol and effectively barring further progress. It was clear that now we had to climb the sheer face.

Again we halted for the night. Again we protected ourselves against the cold with a mighty blaze. As I lay in front of the fire, I pondered on the possible reaction at camp. We were long overdue and they would presume that we were lost. Emergency procedures must be imminent there.

Next morning we woke and stirred stiffly. Despite our fitness we felt the strain of it all. Now we were faced with the problem of the cliff. It was a matter of trial and error. After several abortive efforts we finally hit on the happy, but dangerous, solution of using our entrenching tools to chip finger and footholds in the face of the cliff. It was a very exhausted little party that finally reached the summit.

Running along the mountain ridge away from us in the general direction of Kohima was a track and we lay down along the edges to rest. I allowed the men fifteen minutes to recover their strength, after which we set off on the long march. After covering several miles, a jubilant shout from the leading section indicated that a truck was approaching. As it jolted towards us I saw that it was being driven by the Adjutant – Peter Wickham. Beside him sat another officer who was waving to us in great excitement.

They quickly broke out rations from the back of the truck and we ate ravenously. We noticed that they were both unshaven and, as tea was brewing, Peter Wickham explained how they had patrolled all night along the top of the ridge, with headlamps full on and blowing the horn at intervals for our benefit. They guessed that we would strike the track at some point, but of course they could not guess where or when.

Refreshed and heartened, with the last lap in view, we resumed our march back to camp, enriched with experience of both jungle and mountain.

Our camp lay along a mountain track approached by a series of hairpin bends. The tents themselves lay scattered about the crest of the mountain and the ground fell away steeply into a deep valley. The view was superb, with row upon row of purple hills stretching away to the east, towards Burma. It was through these Naga Hills, portions of which even in those days had been unexplored, that the Japanese had moved, intending to overwhelm the small garrison at Kohima. Their secret march so nearly succeeded. Wisps of cloud floated by below the level of our eyes and drifted down the valley, whilst the peaks were wreathed in mists as evening fell.

These hills are peopled by the head-hunting Naga tribesmen, but the ones around Kohima were friendly and always cheerful. They made excellent allies whose labour force had helped to construct the vital supply line from Dimapur to Imphal, known as the Kohima Road to thousands of old soldiers who travelled it during those fateful years.

One of the Naga paths ran straight through our camp. Generations had used it and a few tents were not likely to deter them now. It was a regular sight to see an old Naga, wrapped in his red blanket and clutching his staff, grunting up that path. Following him would come the women with their cone-shaped baskets on their backs, piled high with bamboo and the inevitable flask of zu, or rice wine, sticking out of the top. Very often one would spy the round, brown face and black soft eyes of a baby in the basket, regarding with wonder the strange people who had appeared in their midst.

They were a primitive race, whose language seemed to bear no relationship to any other. After studying Urdu and Gurkhali, one could generally follow the form of most of the other dialects of India even if one could not translate them; but to hear the Naga tongue conveyed nothing. To our ears it seemed to consist mostly of grunts and gabble. One of the officers attached to us had passed through this country during the 1942 Retreat when serving with a British regiment. He was alone, exhausted and near the end of his tether when the Nagas picked him up. They fed him and gave him shelter in a village from the probing eyes of Japanese patrols. He had a little notebook in which he had attempted to write up their language, with some success. Whilst with us he would sometimes slip away in his spare time to visit them in their villages and to receive a warm welcome.

As I watched these Nagas passing to and fro, I thought of the strange coincidence that had brought a battalion of the 8th Gurkha Rifles to Kohima in this year – 1944. Our regimental history shows that, between 1839 and 1913, our regiment was engaged in many expeditions amongst these same hills, against stockaded villages, usually perched on mountain tops, until the whole of Manipur was pacified. At Kohima itself a stone memorial stands on ground once occupied by the barracks of the Assam Rifles before the war and now occupied by a hospital. The memorial is dedicated to those officers and men who fell in action during those wars of the last century. It was with a shock that I deciphered an inscription on the tablet carved out over fifty years previously.

This hospital was staffed by the same sisters whom I had met at the rest camp at Dimapur. They had come back to Kohima when the Japs had retreated and there they carried on their good work. Sally was also there and occasionally I would visit the hospital to see her and to renew our acquaintance.

Needless to say, my trips did not go unnoticed and one day the Colonel suggested that I and some of my fellow officers who also liked to visit the hospital should invite the sisters to a party. This idea appealed immensely to all of us and we lost no time in making the necessary arrangements.

The idea of entertaining our guests caught our imaginations and it was decided to improve our mess tent for the occasion. With the aid of the transport officer we removed the tarpaulin roof from the jeep stand and this was transformed into a floor covering in the mess; we normally had no covering on the grass floor of this tent. Owing to the extreme cold in the evenings at that height someone suggested that we might build a fireplace to impress and to coddle the ladies. Bricks were discovered from I know not where and a passable imitation of an English cottage fireplace gradually grew under the supervision of a self-appointed expert. The chimney consisted of flattened biscuit tins moulded to the desired shape. Some thirty minutes before the guests arrived a match was applied to the heaped log fire. All present sat back to enjoy the blaze.

In no time we were all coughing and spluttering as bank upon bank of dense black smoke belched out impartially from both brickwork and chimney. Before long the whole of the upper part of the tent was obscured by the resulting haze and we were all scurrying about, bent double, eyes streaming, trying to fan the smoke out of the tent flaps. Panic set in and finally we were obliged to raise the whole of the side-wall of the tent to rid ourselves of the obnoxious, billowing cloud. As the smoke rushed out, the cold rushed in. With only minutes to spare, conditions returned to normal and we were able to greet the arrivals with sang-froid. The fireplace remained a useless ornament for the rest of our stay there. Perhaps it now forms part of a Naga cookhouse?

The party itself was a success. Mike Tidswell, whom I had known in Quetta, produced a banjo and entertained us all with great gusto; the ladies seemed to enjoy their visit and on the strength of it all we invited them to come at a later date to see a Gurkha Nautch (dance). This was arranged by the Gurkhas themselves and proved fascinating to our visitors.

Not far from us, down our mountain track, the 1/11th Sikh Regiment and the King's Own Scottish Borderers had their own separate camps. Together, we formed 89 Indian Infantry Brigade of the 7th Indian Division. The division was known colloquially as 'The Golden Arrow Div' because of the insignia which we wore on our shoulder flashes. This mixture of British, Indian and Gurkha troops in one brigade was most successful. Each regiment had its own particular national characteristics; each respected and admired the others; each, either in the past or the future, was called upon to come to the aid of the others in action; the brigade was to prove a match for the Imperial Japanese Army.

During our stay in Kohima, despite the intensive training, we had our breaks for recreation and our more light-hearted moments. One of our favourite sports was to play basketball against the Sikhs. This game was quite a favourite in the Indian Army. Anyone could level a pitch in a jungle clearing, fit up two posts and mark out a square. The game itself was no patball and was always played with extreme vigour and skill.

The sight of the tall, bearded Sikhs, with their black hair coiled in a bun on top of their heads, competing with the stocky, agile Gurkhas was a lesson in contrast. The Sikhs would play the open game, with the long pass lobbed from end to end, whilst our men would favour the short pass, from hand to hand like a bunch of Rugby forwards sweeping down the field. The fact that they disappeared from time to time amongst the long legs of the Sikhs would cause great amusement amongst the spectators, but did not prevent them from bobbing up to score their opportunist goals.

After these games, in which we all joined, we got to know the Sikh officers particularly well. They were mostly British, but there were several Sikhs amongst them who held the King's Commission. They were a merry bunch, always ready for some tomfoolery.

When morale is high, spirits are high and many were the antics in which we indulged. I well remember one episode when we accepted a challenge to a mule race. Mounted bareback on our steeds, we dashed around and around a course laid out on the grass, some perched on their rumps, others hugging their necks with apparent affection until most riders ended up in the laps of the onlookers. The winner was our venerable Subadar-Major who stuck on his mule but whose critics suggested that his portly weight was causing the poor mule more embarrassment than its normal full load of ammunition.

Just before Christmas, our training and our rest came to an abrupt end. The Colonel called a conference of all officers and it was with a rising sense of excitement that we grouped ourselves around him.

He did not mince words.

A map of the Burma front showed that at that moment the battle for Mandalay was mounting in ferocity; obviously the Japs had their main forces in possession of the city to deny it to the Fourteenth Army.

After reading out a most stirring Order of the Day* which called upon us for a final effort to destroy the Japanese forces in Burma, Colonel Walker looked us over with a searching glance and spoke.

'We of IV Corps,' he said, 'have been given the task of outflanking Mandalay by means of a tremendous right hook. The operation is utterly secret and when we move there will be complete wireless silence.'

He paused.

'Our first objective is Pakokku, on the banks of the Irrawaddy.'

Several of those present could not suppress a gasp of astonishment. Pakokku! The Irrawaddy River! A glance at the map showed that this Burmese town lay some 450 miles away, and was situated a hundred miles south of Mandalay, virtually behind the Japanese lines.

* Reproduced as an appendix to this book on page 189.

'Our brigade is to move off first,' he continued, 'and we have been given the honour of leading the brigade. We shall be twenty-four hours ahead of the brigade and, of course, normal means of supply are out of the question. We shall be supplied from the air.'

A buzz of excitement immediately ran around our group. Here was news indeed. Here was goodbye to the training routine with a vengeance. 450 miles on 'Air drop'. What a prospect!

The Colonel continued:

'I have been watching you all during these last few weeks. Owing to reinforcements and changes we are virtually a fresh battalion and like a fresh battalion your spirit is high. I know each of you personally; I know your good points and I know your faults. After this conference is over, I propose to interview each one of you. I shall tell you what I think of you and your capabilities. The rest is up to you.'

He was as good as his word.

Later that day, I found myself standing outside the Colonel's tent, at a discreet distance, in quiet conversation with one or two of my brother officers. I had seen the varying expressions on the faces of those who had already undergone their interview: some thoughtful; some grim; some poker-faced. The thought of hearing this keen soldier's personal assessment of my capabilities was distinctly unsettling.

An officer stepped out of the tent and beckoned me. Gritting my teeth, I ducked under the tent flap, came to attention and saluted. Colonel Walker was sitting at a trestle table, with some papers before him. It was early evening and a hurricane lamp standing on the bare boards cast a soft glow about the tent; the faint smell of paraffin permeated the air.

'You've been with us for a month or two now, Denis?'

'Yes, Sir.'

'Do you like the battalion?'

'Certainly, Sir. I have met several officers I knew in Quetta and quite a few of the recruits passed through my hands there.'

'That's fine,' he continued, 'because from to-night I want you to take over command of "B" Company.' He rose to his feet and held out his hand. 'Congratulations, *Major* Sheil-Small.'

I was staggered. The CO went on to run over details of 'B'

Company but I hardly took in what he was saying. Not only was this news overwhelming; it was also disturbing. I was new to the battalion and I had not been in action. I was perfectly confident about all the training which I had absorbed in the training centre and at a battle inoculation course at the Jungle Warfare Training School at Saugor. In the training centre I had commanded a company of recruits, as a captain, and I was in no doubt about my ability to pass on that training. But none of it was the real thing. This was different. Now I was being asked to lead into battle a company of whom the majority had already been blooded. What if I failed?

I had already nursed a secret sense of satisfaction in being second-in-command to Peter Myers, to whom I would be looking for example under fire. Everyone who has been to war knows this feeling. The experience of those who have been under fire seems to set them apart as a select band. Their vivid accounts impel respect and even if we suspect, in some, that time has magnified the event, we do not begrudge the telling but rather accept it as their due.

Now my bubble of satisfaction had burst.

I would have to find it all out for myself, and in the finding, be expected to show example to these splendid men.

The Colonel sensed my confusion and put a kindly hand on my shoulder.

'The Gurkhas are excellent soldiers,' he said, 'but they've got to be resolutely led. Have faith in yourself, Denis, and they will have faith in you. I am putting my trust in you. I can do no more. Good luck.'

I saluted and, stooping, passed out of the tent.

When I joined the others in the mess tent, it was with mixed feelings. They were one and all boisterous in their congratulations. Peter Myers went to his tent and returned with a pair of shoulder straps embossed with black crowns. 'You had better waste no time in putting these on,' he said.

After the celebrations in the mess, I retired to the tent occupied by Captain Toby Wilcox, from whom I was taking over command of 'B' Company. Toby was a personal friend of mine and I found it was somewhat embarrassing to have to supersede him. We talked far into the night. I learned of the platoon commanders, the section commanders and, above all, of the riflemen. Familiar names cropped up as we ran through the list of NCOs in the company, and their personal histories.

In a Gurkha regiment, the names repeat themselves endlessly – the Lalbahadur Gurungs, The Purne Puns, the Jitbahadur Thapas, the Durge Ales – there were dozens with the same name. To identify them of course there were the regimental numbers allocated to each one, but we always preferred the personal touch. We thought of them as Lalbahadur the runner, Lalbahadur the boxer, Jitbahadur the hockey player, Jitbahadur the footballer, and so on.

I fell asleep later that night with a kaleidoscope of runners, jumpers and boxers flickering behind my tired eyelids.

CHAPTER THREE
Into Burma

We were now in Christmas week and the order to move was published for 23rd December. This gave us just one more day at Kohima.

I set off for my last trip to the hospital where Sally was delighted to hear of my promotion, but saddened by the impending move. We said our farewells and parted reluctantly, both wondering whether we would ever meet again. Neither of us was under any misapprehension about what lay ahead.

As my jeep passed through Kohima I took my last look at this place which I had come to know so well and whose name has since become immortal. I stood again at the very spot where my truck had halted on that first day when I passed through to join my battalion. At the road junction, set back from the Imphal-Dimapur road itself, in a semi-circle of grey stone there now stands the monument raised to honour the dead whose graves are marked by row upon row of white crosses, each bearing its poignant inscription.

Engraved upon the stone of the monument are the moving words which carry a message far beyond the battle of Kohima and which have come to honour all who fell in the Fourteenth Army, throughout the length and breadth of Burma:

'When you go Home, tell them of us and say
That for their to-morrow we gave our today.'

Moving upwards off the road, I passed amongst the shell-torn trees, with their newly budding foliage and the green shadows were around me. In turn, I came to the memorials to the Welch Fusiliers – a plain white stone surmounted by the regimental Black Flash;

the simple cross of the Queen's Royal Regiment and, crossing the ground where the Royal West Kents made their famous stand and Lance-Corporal John Harman won his Victoria Cross posthumously, I saw the charred remains of the District Commissioner's bungalow where the British and Japanese infantry divided the garden between their opposing forces; so close were they that a Japanese soldier deepening his foxhole inadvertently threw a shovelful of earth into a British trench. The slaughter, the horror and the shambles of it all became clear to me and I looked again at the terrace upon terrace of those white crosses, the final evidence of the sacrifice of the defenders of Kohima.

My eyes moved from the graves to Kohima Ridge and on to the heights of Naga Village, with the lone Highlander. My gaze travelled over the whole scene and I thought of those regiments who had fought and died and for whom there stood no memorials at all – the Gurkhas, the Indians and the other British regiments, whose only memorials were the stirring deeds which they performed when the Gateway to India was slammed full in the faces of the advancing Japanese horde.

I wondered whether they would all be looking down on us in the coming advance, and whether they would ever learn that their sacrifice was not in vain.

It was dark and the convoy of trucks and lorries stretched away along the road, at their set intervals, until the column disappeared around the bend of the track behind us. Ahead, the vehicles of 'A' Company were faintly discernible as I gave my last orders to my platoon commanders. It was 23rd December 1944, and we were about to embus for our momentous journey which was finally to end with the overthrow of the Japanese in Burma, at the cost of the lives of so many of us and the pain and suffering of the wounded who survived.

We mounted, and as I sat beside the driver of my truck, waiting to move off, I cast my eyes over the ground we had vacated. Our tents had vanished and from now on we were to live in home-made bashas or holes in the ground. In place of the camp we had come to know so well lay the bare hillside which, in retaining its natural form, was somehow alien to our eyes.

I wondered what the Nagas would say, next morning, when they came grunting up their path to find nothing but the imprint of our tents on the grass. Would our coming and going assume the shape of a legend in the days to come? Would old men around the camp fires at the turn of the century look into the flames and describe to the youngsters how the Big War raged amongst the valleys and the hills? Would they speak of the slant-eyed troops who marched out of the jungle one day to camp on their hill and who vanished, as suddenly, one dark night? Who knows?

My reverie was broken as the lorry in front of us shuddered into life, and we were off.

After travelling for about twenty minutes along our track, I discerned the vague outlines of the huts of Kohima and we rumbled through the silent dwellings to the road junction and turned our noses south towards the Imphal Plain.

All throughout the night we drove, the road descending steadily as mile after mile slipped past. Usually the motion of a truck lulls one into a sort of coma and many of the slouch-hatted heads in the body of the truck were nodding in salute to sleep, that blessed alleviator of aches, ills and pains. On this occasion, however, my eyes were wide awake and my brain alert and occupied with many thoughts.

Every inch of this road was historical. Carved out of a mere track, it had been created with the aid of the Assam Tea Garden Labour Force and the Naga tribesmen, until it became an engineering wonder. Three vehicles could easily manoeuvre abreast of each other, except on the hairpin bends. These bends themselves were carried by culverts across countless ravines. The Japs had methodically destroyed culvert after culvert and bridge after bridge, but each had been patiently repaired and was in use again.

My mind wandered back to the previous year when I attended a course of instruction at the Army Tactical School, Poona. One of the young student officers gave a lecture to the rest of us about this part of the Front, before the Japs crossed the Chindwin River. He described how some of Wingate's men, after their ordeal in Burma, had made their way back. Some of the groups had actually debouched on to this road – the very road they had travelled down from railhead in 1943 at the start of their famous expedition. I looked out of the cab window and wondered just what part they had struck.

During the early part of the night it was pitch dark, and it was the continual changing down of the gears and the resulting protesting whine of the engine that proclaimed our downward progress. Later, however, the moon rose – a true Burma moon – huge, majestic and hanging low in the sky. As the brilliance grew, the whole countryside took shape before my eyes. The scenery was no less beautiful by night than by day, and I was quite fascinated by the panorama. The mountain peaks on our flanks appeared gradually to give way to foothills which, in turn, receded. Suddenly, we were out of the hills and into the Imphal Plain of 600 square miles, the 'Bloody Plain' where the spine of the Imperial Japanese Army in south-east Asia was broken, at a cost of 60,000 dead.

At the southern end of the plain, around Bishenpur, the Japs had directed their shock troops to break through at all costs and the Japanese 33rd Division had met head-on with the 17th Indian Division. For days and nights the killing had gone on, without retreat by either side, as these divisions were old enemies. In that fighting alone three Victoria Crosses were won by British and Gurkha soldiers.

It was here in this plain that General Slim and his three corps commanders were knighted by the Viceroy of India, as the shattered Japanese army withdrew and started their long retreat down to the Irrawaddy River.

As we drove on, the moon which was now a ball of orange light dropped behind the hills as suddenly as it had risen; once more we were enveloped in a pall of blackness. When dawn came finally, the first faint glimmer of the rising sun appeared almost to push out fingers of ice across the sky, in contrast to the Burma moon.

We crossed the plain in daylight, passing through Imphal and resuming our journey southward. My total knowledge of Imphal is confined to those fleeting glances from a moving truck; it appeared to be a more civilized town than the little hill station of Kohima.

On and on we journeyed, down to Palel through the area where our sister battalion, the 3/8th Gurkha Rifles, had fought its own battles as part of the 20th Indian Division. We now climbed again, up through the Chin Hills and down the Palel-Tamu road which had been built originally to help to extricate our retreating army from Burma in 1942.

As the Japanese commander, General Kimura, drew back his decimated divisions, the 11th East African Division and the Allied close support Air Forces hammered the Japs all the way down to Tamu. It was on this road that evidence was found that the Japanese failure to capture Imphal and Kohima had written their own sentence of starvation and death on the road back. Wrecked transport wagons by the score were found with skeletons sitting at the wheel. Japanese staff cars rusted there with several grim passengers apiece; many more lay by the roadside or on tracks with their hands behind their heads, as though asleep. Their flesh had been eaten by white ants.

We entered Tamu on Christmas Eve.

The air reeked of disaster and death. The roads were ankle deep in thick dust, churned up in choking clouds by huge tank transporters overtaken by our convoy. The sight of our own tanks was heartening and we had cause to bless them later when we came to grips with the Japanese. The trees and jungle at the side of the road were plastered white by the dust and bore little resemblance to nature, but rather looked like vast artificial stage props. Here and there on each flank were huge notices nailed to trees, with warnings, in English and Urdu, to beware of mines and booby-traps. Several times we passed the twisted and rusted remains of Japanese vehicles, exactly where their owners had perished.

This was the jungle of the story books. All about us immense teak trees rose up to a height of some seventy feet or more, completely dwarfing ourselves and our transport. The trunks of the trees were utterly bare from base to top, where they blossomed out into huge leaves and foliage which intermingled from tree to tree, forming a canopy that excluded the sun, except in clearings where its rays pierced the gloom like sunbeams slanting through a cathedral window. At ground level, the intervals between the trees presented a tangled mass of creepers and undergrowth which caught at your clothes as you passed by.

We took up our dispositions in these new surroundings, with the various companies quite independently sited away from the battalion headquarters. One of the first things I noticed was the echo of voices; in the jungle, sound effects were not unlike the booming of sound reflected by the canopied roof of a large railway terminus.

The chopping of wood as kukris were put to use to build bashas, the shouts and laughter of the Gurkhas as they went about their many tasks of settling in were magnified enormously in a way so startlingly different from our quiet mountain camp. I thought to myself that we should need extreme self-discipline when we came into close contact with the enemy in such surroundings. I understood at last the tales of the jungle, where the snapping of a twig rings out like a shot and warns the hunted of the presence of the hunter. It was clear to me that such tales were not exaggerated after all.

That night, as I lay in my sleeping bag and our human activities had lapsed into silence, I became aware of a new sound. All night long I could hear the steady plop at irregular intervals as of huge raindrops falling about us, and I was puzzled. The sound was not regular and could not, therefore, be rain. In any case, it was not the monsoon season. After listening for some time, I stuck my head out into the open and cocked my ears. It suddenly dawned upon me that what I was hearing was the condensation of moisture forming huge drops of water which fell the odd seventy feet from the trees to crash amongst the undergrowth or slap onto the hard, shiny surface of the tropical plants. An unhealthy-looking mist seemed to rise from the earth. I shivered and stuck my head down deep into my bag, wishing devoutly that I had a tent to cover me.

Next morning, as I opened my eyes, the smiling face of my orderly hovered over my mosquito net as he pushed a mug of hot tea into my hand. With the air of a conjuror, he produced hot water in my mess tin and I started to shave, squinting into my steel mirror. As I looked at my face, almost unfamiliar in the grey dawn, a thought suddenly struck me. This was Christmas Day!

After the ablutions, there was a score of things to be done. Orders regarding rations; digging of slit trenches; digging of latrines; checking of ammunition; inspection of weapons. All the routine of active service conditions required attention. I had been given to understand that whilst at Tamu the British officers would

Assault Course. Battle Training.

Assault Course. Battle Training.

Quetta, 1943 (winter). Second-Lieutenants Bob Prentice and Mike Tidswell (later killed in Burma at Taungdaw).

Quetta, 1943 (winter). Major Dawson, Lieutenant Thomas, Second-Lieutenants Quentin Kennedy and Mike Tidswell. (Both killed in Burma 1945.)

be taking meals for a change in a central basha at Headquarters. In due course, satisfied that things were under control, I set off for my breakfast.

Setting off through the jungle, I had not travelled more than fifty yards when I got a shock. For the life of me I could not tell in which direction lay my objective; furthermore, the noises which echoed so loudly in the immediate vicinity of the company position were now utterly blanketed even at this short distance by the trees. One does not usually reckon to use a compass to guide one to one's breakfast, even in the jungle, but I had to face the fact that I was as good as lost. I pressed on hopefully, feeling extremely lonely, and more by luck than judgement finally arrived at my destination. It was an early lesson in jungle warfare.

The day was given over to settling in, but we did celebrate Christmas Dinner in as good a style as we could muster. The Gurkhas had cheerfully wielded their kukris to good effect amongst the trees and had fashioned a table and two wooden benches for our use. Luxuries such as plates and crockery had vanished, however, and from now on it was messtins at mealtimes. Inevitably, my mind flashed back to the previous Christmas Day which I had spent in the very civilized atmosphere of the Regimental Training Centre. With a touch of nostalgia, I recalled the gleaming silver, the plates embossed with the regimental crest, the snowy, crisp napkins, the impressive silver statuettes and trophies standing down the length of the polished mahogany table. I remembered the regimental pipers marching into the dining room, the beauty of the pipe banners and the deafening skirl of the pipes as they marched round and round in that confined space. I could taste the port and smell the cigar smoke. Further back went my mind, as, in a reverie, I recalled other Christmases spent in the peace and comfort of my own home, surrounded by parents, brothers and sisters.

With Christmas over, we settled down to business in earnest.

For two weeks we stayed at Tamu, practising and perfecting the art of killing. Daily, a large part of the training was devoted to Kukri and bayonet fighting. The jungle echoed to blood-curdling yells and cries as platoon after platoon carried out bayonet charges en masse, and hacked and lunged at individual dummies representing Japanese. What we called 'The Rifleman's Creed' was dinned into the Gurkhas at every opportunity. This consisted of a series of slogans which were learned by heart and on which they would be questioned by NCO, Gurkha officer or British officer. I cannot remember them all after the passage of nearly forty years, but a few will remain in my memory for the rest of my days. The English translations are as follows:

'It is the ambition of every man of the 4/8th Gurkha Rifles to redden his kukri and bayonet in Japanese blood.'

'One bullet – one Japanese.'

'Live hard, fight hard, and if necessary, die hard.'

'Our Regiment never retires without orders.'

It is not, perhaps, a strange thing that when I became involved in my first battle and the numbness of surprise at a sudden onslaught threatened to paralyse my reactions, the slogans of the creed sprang to my tongue as I shouted to my men to encourage them.

The NCOs had their own creed; amongst the slogans I remember:

'Camouflage is not enough; my men must be invisible.'

'In any situation, the one unforgiveable crime is inaction. Therefore, if I have no orders, I must think what my commander would wish me to do – and act accordingly.'

During the intensified training in which we were now engaged, we were encouraged to find our way about the jungle, and company stalked company in mock attacks.

CHAPTER FOUR

Jungle Punishment

During these last two weeks the battalion was being tuned up deliberately by the CO, in the same way that a trainer brings a boxer to the height of physical perfection, just before he enters the ring.

There is no doubt that discipline is the key to success in soldiering, and the Colonel was never a laggard in imposing it. As the days went by, he increased the pressure and one episode will serve to illustrate his utter impartiality as between officers and men.

A conference had been arranged for all British officers at HQ for 0900 hours on a particular morning. It was to be held in the mess basha. Now it is an unwritten law in the Army that one shall be on parade five minutes before the advertised time of parade, and we might have been excused perhaps for losing sight of this nicety in our primitive jungle surroundings. In any case, as I have already explained, the trip to Headquarters from our different company areas called for quite a minor navigational feat.

I was a few minutes late, as were two officers from other companies. We entered the basha to find everyone already seated on the bamboo benches and the Colonel presiding. We made our conventional apologies and took our seats. The Colonel looked at his watch and spoke very quietly:

'Gentlemen,' he said, 'As you know, a Gurkha regiment is renowned for discipline. So far, you have ably assisted me lately in gearing the men up to exactly the right pitch.'

His voice rose in pitch: 'How the devil can we expect discipline from the men if their officers cannot keep to a simple timetable. I *will* have punctuality!'

We all knew Walter Walker well enough by this time to sense an implied threat. All during the discussions and orders the three of us felt uncomfortable, like schoolboys awaiting an imposition. The CO clearly meant what he said, and yet no punishment had been imposed. I, for one, wondered at the back of my mind what he could do. A reprimand would be official, but rather pointless as we had already been 'rocketed' in front of the others. You cannot be 'confined to your quarters' in the jungle, and under present active service conditions. So what sort of punishment remained?

As the meeting drew to a close, the CO returned to his theme.

'I have been thinking about you three', he said, with a cold stare, and I propose to set you an exercise in punctuality.'

We looked up in puzzled anticipation.

'I shall place a notebook in each company guard basha and also here in Battalion HQ. After Stand-to this evening, each of you will commence to tour these guard posts; you will place your signatures, in turn, in all these books together with a note of time of signature. You will continue to do so until the dawn Stand-to. All sentries will be warned so that none of you will get shot during your tours.'

Later that day an orderly handed me a slip of paper upon which was written the times at which we individually had to sign the books. It worked out at three-hourly intervals throughout the night. This seemed severe to me but I did not realise the full implications until I had my first taste of it.

That evening the usual dusk stand-to took place at about 1800 hours. In those parts night comes early and it comes fast. We took up our defensive positions in the fading light, complete with equipment and weapons to hand. In utter silence we waited as the jungle gloom gave way to darkness. In due course we stood down and broke up into little groups to chat quietly before turning in.

An officer from 'A' Company was due to make the first tour to sign the books; I was to commence mine at 1900 hours. I squatted down by my sleeping bag and awaited his call. At about 1850 he appeared and told me that it was very difficult to find the various company areas. I thought of my own adventure the morning that I nearly got lost on my way to breakfast in broad daylight and I did not relish trying the same game in darkness. He wished me good luck and set off towards his own company. I warned my subadar who was nearby that I was about to leave the company perimeter and stressed the fact that I did not want to get shot by a zealous Gurkha on my return. I then walked down the track and cut off into the jungle.

The trees seemed closer together than ever and I strained my eyes to focus in the dark. The ground was uneven and, apart from creepers that seemed to snake out of the undergrowth, my boots kept slipping on jungle roots which surfaced underfoot for yards at a time before dipping back into the dank earth. The human sense of balance is very delicate indeed and I have often noticed, on night marches and patrols, how uneven going destroys your equilibrium and calls for so much extra effort in counter-balance.

I stumbled along, grateful at least that this was not a real patrol into Jap territory but merely an 'exercise in punctuality'. It was easy to let the imagination loose and to visualise the battle which had passed through these forests, with the green shadows flitting from tree to tree in pursuit of the enemy.

I found 'C' Company when a Gurkha sentry rose out of the deeper shadows and challenged me as I was about to step on him. Our sentries were always prone the better to see a Jap outline silhouetted against the night sky. I gave the password and was taken to the guard commander. This havildar (sergeant) produced the book and stood respectfully by me as I signed it, as if it was perfectly natural for a Sahib to turn up out of the jungle in the night just to sign a little book. It certainly took something to surprise a Gurkha. I thanked him and set off to find the next company.

I finally completed my round and, having awakened the third wrong-doer, got back to my own sleeping bag feeling quite tired and lost no time in getting my head down; it was of course quite pointless to remove my clothes. No sooner had I dropped off, so it seemed, than Scott Gilmore was shaking me into wakefulness for my second session. I looked at my watch; it was 2300 hours.

Scott departed for his own bed, and I set off on my second round. This time mist had enveloped the whole forest and my teeth fairly chattered with the cold, as I pressed on through the wet vegetation, the only sound being the plop of the drops of moisture falling from the trees. I managed to make the rounds without incident, but when at last I stumbled into my sleeping bag my eyes felt red and sore with peering into the darkness. The strain was beginning to make itself felt. I thought ruefully of a character back in the training centre who used to look around the breakfast table after a Guest Night and comment on the revellers whose eyes, in his view, looked as if they 'had receded a couple of monsoon seasons.'

I awoke with a start to find Scott Gilmore bending over me. What, already? In the reflected beam of his torch, shining on my face, his eyes looked shrunken and bloodshot. 'Wakey! Wakey!' he croaked, 'Last round – good luck.' I hauled myself onto my feet and set off like an automaton.

Next morning, three chastened and very bleary-eyed officers sat down to breakfast (punctually) and failed to see the humour in the remarks which greeted their arrival in the mess.

The news that three officer-sahibs had actually been punished went round the ranks like wild fire and wherever we appeared that day they eyed us with interest but with smiles of renewed affection.

Even now we did not realize that this punishment was to be repeated for three succeeding nights, but the CO gave no sign of absolving us. At the end of this time we felt completely shattered. Added to the physical discomfort was the nagging thought that soon the battalion would be setting off for the big advance into Burma, and we really needed all the sleep we could get.

On the third morning we stumbled into breakfast. The CO looked us over, with the remark that our days at Tamu were now numbered.

'I think that you gentlemen had better get some sleep to-night,' he said, 'The brigade will shortly be on the move. By the way, I do hope that you have learned a lesson.'

That night I enjoyed the finest night's sleep that I could ever remember.

It is generally supposed that troops in jungle are often surrounded by wild animals and reptiles. This might be true of some out of the way training areas. However, where fighting has taken place, the wild life of the area has usually fled in panic in front of the invaders of the solitude, who are bent on destroying each other.

I don't know whether snakes are more tenacious than animals in this respect, but they were the one form of wild life which we came across regularly, both at Tamu and, later, in Burma where the

Central Plain (H.E. Bates's 'Purple Plain') resembles a desert. The particular inhabitant of the Tamu jungle was the krait, a tiny yellow snake no longer than six inches, but whose bite is reckoned to be fatal. We saw plenty of these and I was concerned myself in one incident which still makes me shudder when I think of it.

My orderly had constructed for me a small sleeping platform of bamboo which was raised some six inches off the ground. It was of just sufficient height to free me from contact with the damp ground and its ill-humoured night mists. My sleeping bag rested on the top and my mosquito-net, upheld by two small vertical posts, would be tucked in all around it.

One night I was particularly restless and when at last I fell into a fitful slumber I dreamed of snakes. They were of all lengths and colours, but the small, yellow kraits seemed to predominate in the dream. There was no apparent reason for such a dream, and when daylight came at last I dismissed the nightmare as a phantasy associated, in a Freudian sort of way, with the mepacrine tablets we were taking every evening, resulting in our yellow complexions under our brown tan.

A little while later, as I bent over my canvas bucket to wash the sleep out of my eyes, I heard a commotion and the voice of my orderly raised in triumph. I looked up and nearly cut myself with my razor as he came bounding up dangling two yellow kraits from a forked stick. It took me a minute to realize that their heads were smashed in. Jitbahadur pointed excitedly to my sleeping bag which he had turned back, preparatory to rolling it up, and showed me where the reptiles had been curled up on the bamboo platform under the bag, sharing with me the warmth which it afforded.

Laughing immoderately, he bore them off to the battalion doctor who took a professional interest in all snakes at all times. I think he learned more during his association with us than from any School of Tropical Medicine. In Central Burma we produced a motley collection for him, including the deadly Russell's Viper, with its mottled dark blue and green colouring. One of my NCOs quietly squatting in his slit trench and watching his front on a dark night, for signs of Jap activity, suddenly discovered that he shared the trench with one of these vipers. He despatched it with his kukri, but the story does not reveal whether he lay down to sleep there when his relief took over.

One of the most notorious species of snake in that part of the world was the King Cobra. Rising out of the Central Plain, south of Mandalay, there is a large mountain – Mount Popa. The environment of this majestic bulk was the home of this deadly snake. Later in the campaign there was bitter fighting around this area; those who took part had hair-raising tales of chasing the Japs in and out of rocks, boulders and caves swarming with these reptiles.

Before we left Tamu, I saw my first python. A sharp-eyed Gurkha had spotted him right up at the top of one of the tall teak trees and quite a discussion ensued about the best method of dealing with him. His body was curled around the main trunk and blended most beautifully with the background. His evil-looking head had betrayed his presence as it quested back and forth, in search of a victim.

I knew that the Company Havildar-Major (Company Sergeant-Major) was our best rifle shot and I told him to go ahead and shoot. He crouched down in the kneeling position, steadied himself, took careful aim and fired one shot. It was a beauty. I could see the snake's head jerk up as the .303 bullet smashed into it; slowly the huge coils relaxed their grip on the tree and unwound as the snake slithered down to the ground.

The doctor was delighted with this latest acquisition and even talked grandly about having it preserved. However, next day the battalion received orders to move and the general excitement drove all else clean out of our heads.

CHAPTER FIVE

The Bloody River

On 8th January 1945 we left Tamu and moved by truck and route march to a village named Inthe, some fifty miles north of Gangaw, on the right bank of the Myttha River. From here the advance commenced.

As we had learned, before leaving Kohima, we were to lead the 89th Indian Infantry Brigade in a long left flanking movement through the hills to the banks of the Irrawaddy – a march of several hundred miles, all of it on foot. We ourselves were to be the spearhead and move one day's march ahead of the brigade. Supply would be from the air. Together with a Mountain Battery of the Royal Artillery and a platoon of the Indian Engineers, we were christened 'A' Column. We set off on 18th January.

We first moved down to Gangaw, a town that had been captured by the Lushai Brigade, and from there we had a leg of one hundred and fifty miles in front of us before we would reach the Irrawaddy. African troops here had been held up by the Japanese and we were given the task of moving secretly through the hills and jungle to cut the road in their rear, between Tilin and Pauk, and to capture Pauk itself. Success in this venture would isolate the Japanese opposition.

As we set off, we were told to expect trouble and we advanced down the road in battle formation, scouts out, and with cocked rifles. It was after passing through the last African outposts that we became the southernmost troops in Burma at that particular time. It certainly tightened the stomach muscles to realise that, as we edged forward, we were now quite literally the tip of the spearhead piercing the Japanese flank.

The going was hard and our efforts unflagging over the primitive tracks. Where we went, the mules followed and it was necessary in places to cut a track for them. Behind them, willing hands carved out a track for the vehicles of the division which moved at our heels.

Each day we were on our feet at dawn, with a daily stint of some fifteen miles ahead of us and speed the keynote. As the whole operation depended on secrecy, divisional signs were blacked out and the use of wireless forbidden. We would press on, mile after mile, with one immediate object in mind – to arrive in time at the pre-arranged dropping zone for our air supplies.

We marched mostly by day and sometimes by night; we became hardened to the steady pace of advance and the blisters which had appeared and covered our feet healed themselves. It became a standing joke amongst us that if you dared to show your feet to the doctor he would tear off his own boots and challenge you to produce bigger blisters than his own. Not exactly the perfect bedside manner, but most effective in persuading us to keep our aches and pains to ourselves. An excellent move in psychology.

Without the air drop, all our efforts would have been futile. Those Dakotas, winging their way each day from the supply bases in India to nameless clearings in Burmese jungle and paddyfield, were a sight to behold which never failed to thrill us. As they canted over on one wing to view our smoke signals, we could clearly see the figures, braced in the open hatchways, ready to bundle out their priceless cargoes which would blossom behind them and float to earth, swinging gently under their silken canopies. The fodder for the mules came thudding down without parachutes and bounded and tore its way across the zone, to finish up quite often in the surrounding jungle. There was one ghastly accident during a drop when an enthusiastic rifleman, ignoring shouts to stand clear, rushed in to collect a canister dropped a few moments previously; the tightly-packed bundle of hay hit him fair and square, instantly breaking his neck.

The meticulous planning, the mountains of stores delivered and the perfect timing of the drops all combined to work miracles. I was actually receiving letters from England in a shorter time than they took to reach me at our training centre in Quetta.

Human nature being what it is, we soon became quite blasé and accepted this daily miracle as part of our lives, although, of course, a great deal of work was required on our part. Daily, having reached the dropping zone agreed upon after a hard and gruelling march, we had to set to and clear the ground, lay out the strips and arrange the smoke signals for recognition. All the troops would be deployed on the alert as protection against sudden Japanese attacks as we were now operating in countryside occupied by the Japanese army. That we were unmolested at this particular time was mainly due to our route being far off the beaten track.

In some of the smaller villages we came across, the Burmese there had seen neither British nor Japanese troops since about 1942. They regarded us in amazement, with open mouths, as we debouched silently from the jungle to enter their villages which had been carefully studied by our leading scouts. In other villages the Headman would come out to greet us politely, but with reserve. I well remember one particular individual who approached us and, placing his hands together as if in prayer, rose on his toes as he bowed from the waist. It was clear to our alert eyes, that he must have been under Jap occupation for years to acquire their peculiar characteristics. As we moved through the village we were offered jars of water to drink in the midday heat; I wondered, afterwards, whether I had been rather overdoing my own suspicions when I waved aside these offers in spite of my thirst, and we pressed on.

The Japs themselves were withdrawing in front of us, and in some of the villages we arrived only some eight to twelve hours behind them. This was all too obvious to us from the filth which they left behind them. We prided ourselves on our field hygiene which was strictly enforced, and we were revolted by the evidence which we came across.

To our eager questioning of the villagers as to the whereabouts of the Japanese we always received the same replies – a shake of the head and the stock answer whose translation is roughly 'Japanese? I haven't seen any' or: 'Japanese? They've gone.' The intonation used on these occasions usually also indicated: 'And I don't care'. Looking back, with hindsight, it is easy now to realise that these villagers were terrified of the Japanese; the slightest suspicion of cooperation with us on their part would, if discovered by the Japs, bring down upon their heads the most appalling vengeance. We were to see at first hand, later, the mutilated body of a Burman sprawled in a ditch at the side of the road, having paid the price of displeasing the Japanese masters.

I never learned more than a few simple words in Burmese, but we had with us a few of the Burma Intelligence Corps as interpreters.

These fine men would go off on private forays by themselves and gather invaluable information on which so much of our strategy was based. They were all ex-civilian volunteers, well-educated and from middle-class backgrounds. Every time they set off on their individual forays they took their lives in their hands. It was essential that they should mingle with villagers and peasants and it was not only to the Japs that their lives would be forfeit; there were plenty of traitorous Burmans at that time only too willing to curry favour with the invaders or to seek a reward. Some of the personnel of the Burma Intelligence Corps were to pass within hailing distance of their homes from which they had fled with the Japanese invasion; one can well imagine their feelings after so long away from their hearths. Later, one of them was to save the life of one of our youngest officers by his loyalty and courage under very difficult circumstances when nothing would have been easier than for him quietly to vanish and leave the badly wounded youngster abandoned to his fate.

Our pace was sustained, day after day, amongst hills, along the tracks and through the villages until, at last, we descended the far side of the mountain range and finally reached the Tilin-Pauk road which was our first objective.

After the paths and tracks in the hills, how relieved we were to emerge from the jungle onto this tarmac road, handsome in width and flanked by real telegraph poles which whispered simultaneously of civilisation and of danger. We could easily visualise lorryloads of Japs tearing up and down it, and our ears were permanently cocked for sounds of a vehicle as we crouched by the roadside ditch and made our plans.

The Signals Officer nudged me and pointed to the wires above our heads.

'I'm going up.'

I posted sentries to watch both ways, up and down the road. He shinned up the nearest pole and tapped in on one of the wires with his instrument. After a few moments, listening intently, he shouted down: 'Would you like to hear this?' and threw down the earphones to me. I adjusted them over my head and at once, above the hum of the wires, came the staccato bark of a Japanese conversation.

We now took up a tactical position astride the road and laid a

perfect ambush around the nearest bend. It was a copybook
ambush, sited above and to the side of the road, with a perfect field
of fire for the Bren guns. The far side of the road was then strewn
liberally with mines to destroy any vehicles which would swerve off
the road in their surprise; grenades were put to hand to deal with
any survivors.

Tingling with suspense, we waited.

After about fifteen minutes we heard the faint whine of vehicles
in the distance. Fingers tightened on triggers. I gave the order to
hold fire until my signal. My intention was to get more than one
truck into the killing zone, to inflict maximum casualties.
Suddenly, around the bend came the unmistakeable outline of a
British army truck, complete with painted divisional signs. In my
astonishment, the shout 'Fire' gurgled and died in my throat; the
pent-up breath in my lungs escaped in a long drawn-out sigh.

These were the troops who had originally been held up by the
Japs and on whose behalf we had undertaken our painstaking
journey through those hills. It appeared that the Japs had pulled
out and vanished via side tracks and we found it most galling to
think that it had taken us over a week of marching up hill and down
valley to reach this godforsaken spot which these troops, in their
transport, had reached in a few hours straight down the only
tarmac road in the area. As they went by, raising clouds of dust
from the verges, they made rude signs, laughed and cheered and
jeered good-naturedly; and we, the Poor Bloody Infantry, just
ground our teeth and spat out the dust. Little could they guess how
they had just escaped annihilation.

We learned that night that, in the flush of their new-found
mobility, these same troops rushed straight into a Japanese
ambush farther down the road; all the occupants of the leading jeep
were killed. I saw this vehicle next day, with its shattered
windscreen and rows of bulletholes through the bodywork on both
sides; also, the pathetic cluster of spent cartridge cases on the floor
with their mute evidence of the tommy gunner who had fired back
until his gun was silenced.

This unit was also attacked at night in their bivouacs. Later, I
spoke to a private who had lost his blanket, boots and personal
papers when a small Jap raiding party overran his section position

before being driven back.

Totally on the alert following these incidents, we laid another platoon ambush at a track junction some miles away from our own position. The trap was under the command of the platoon jemadar and it was found necessary, suddenly, to send some urgent information to him.

The Colonel picked upon Toby Wilcox to contact the jemadar and to take command of the ambush. In the emergency he was sent off mounted on one of the chargers that had accompanied our column, in company with the spare mules.

Toby had been in command of the muleteers during the first part of our march and he already had one exciting tale to relate to us concerning his personal adventures. It appeared that as the mules were picking their way along the jungle track, in the dark, a tremendous commotion had convulsed the column as a wild elephant, scenting the alien smell of the mules, had charged through these animals, ripping open the arm of one of the startled Sikh drivers, before crashing off again into the jungle.

I have often remembered his description of his new nightmare journey to the platoon ambush. More than once since then, at regimental reunions, we have laughed at his experience that night, galloping along a tarmac road on a huge horse, in disputed territory, the clatter of hooves ringing out his coming, his carbine slung across his back and bouncing at every jolt, his kukri and bayonet flapping and bumping against the withers of the charger. Even the grenades fell out of his pouches. The only guide he possessed was a map reference; minute by minute he expected the explosion of a Jap ambush.

Coming across a Burman at the side of the road, Toby enquired the way to the nearest village and the man offered his services as a guide. The short cut he chose was a tiger track which cut off some four miles from the straight route. It was so narrow and overgrown that at times they had to crawl on hands and knees but at last they reached the village. Here, Toby was welcomed by the Headman, a venerable old Burman, who greeted him with quite a show of welcome.

'Undoubtedly you have come to collect the horses?' he enquired.

'Horses?' Toby was nonplussed.

'Yes – the horses the Sahib left in our care when the Japanese came and he went away.'

Toby thought quickly. The Japs were here in 1942. If horses had been in the jungle here for some three years then they must be pretty barbary by now. In any case, he was sick of the thought of horses after his nightmare ride.

'Oh, no!' he replied, 'the Sahib will be coming back for the animals himself. I am here to thank you for looking after them and to hear what news you have of the Japanese around here.'

The old man seemed quite content with the reply and gave what information he could about the Japs. Clearly, they were in the district; an ambush should have success, if properly exploited.

Having located the platoon, Toby set about reorganising the lay-out of the sections and, as night fell, they were all ready with their foxholes dug and their weapons covering every possible approach. Sleep was out of the question for anyone; the hours slowly passing seemed an eternity to them all as they crouched in their holes and peered into the darkness.

Just after midnight, a tremendous crashing in the jungle brought rifles into the aim and loosened the pins in grenades. Two enormous dark shapes thundered right through the position and a shrill trumpeting identified them as elephants. They vanished into the distance with a snapping of branches from the trees and silence descended on the platoon. The rest of the night passed without incident. No Japanese were sighted. They were too crafty. They had wind of the ambush and had faded out on unused paths, putting as much distance as possible between themselves and our platoons.

'Don't ever talk to me of mules, chargers or elephants!' Toby used to say to me at subsequent reunions.

We resumed our advance next day but did not come across the enemy. On we journeyed and by 2nd February we had reached the village of Sinthe, thirty miles west of Pakokku, after passing through Pauk a few days earlier.

Three days later, we were favoured with a visit from the Fourteenth Army Commander, General Sir William Slim, accompanied by the IV Corps Commander, Lieutenant-General F.W. Messervy, 7th Indian Division Commander, Major-General

G.C. Evans, and 89 Indian Infantry Brigade Commander, Brigadier W.A. Crowther.

General Slim was very kind in his remarks about our march through the hills and, as we listened, we sensed in him that indefinable quality that marks out the really great leader. The fact that he himself had served in a Gurkha regiment in his young days and spoke Gurkhali of course further endeared him to us all. He had already addressed us at Kohima before we set out and he had pulled no punches. He had told us that our task was to destroy the Japanese army, no less, and that in carrying out that task a large proportion of us would never return; it was the debt which we owed to the country that gave us birth.

Altogether we spent eight days in this area. During that time the battalion helped in the construction of an airfield large enough to serve three divisions.

On 10th February we moved on and during that night we achieved a march which was something of a record. In ten hours we covered twenty-six miles over stretches of soft river beds or chaungs, and a precipitous mountain. There was no moon and the night was pitch black. Each man carried his large pack on his back and a full quota of ammunition. I thought that the end would never come.

As hour after hour went by, the crunch of marching boots beat like a tattoo on the weary brain; the large pack on my back between my shoulder blades assumed monstrous proportions in the black night. After we had marched some twenty miles, I was mortified to find that my left knee was beginning to swell. My mind flashed back over the years to an injury on the Rugby field when I had twisted it very badly. The last six miles found me limping along in a sweat of apprehension lest I should not last the distance.

Frank Crouchman who had marched near me at intervals during the night spotted my difficulties in spite of the dark and insisted, in spite of my protests, on relieving me of my pack for the last leg of the march. In consequence I managed to finish on my feet but felt rather ashamed, although in the darkness very few people realised just what a magnificent gesture Frank had made. I have never forgotten the incident.

The Divisional Commander later sent his congratulations on the

Kohima. The area in the background was the scene of heavy fighting. The hospital is in the foreground.

Christmas at No 53 Indian General Hospital. British sick and wounded. Sally is the Nursing Sister on the left.

(Left) 8th Gurkha Rifles War Memorial at Kohima.

(Below) War Graves at Kohima.

night's efforts, so they must have been impressed by his standards at least.

Next day was to take us to the banks of the Irrawaddy. Before we fell in on the line of march the Colonel approached me and instructed me to accompany Tony Brand Crombie in a jeep as Advance Party, ahead of the column. This was fortunate indeed as my knee gained respite from further immediate strain and never troubled me again during the rest of the campaign. No doubt Intelligence reports must have stated that the area was free of Japs for the Colonel to send two of his officers ahead on their own and without an escort but as far as we were concerned it did give us a creepy feeling at the time.

We completed the distance without incident and, as we came out of the hilly, rocky mountain studded with oil derricks belonging to the Burmah Oil Company on the west bank of the Irrawaddy, we were struck dumb by the beauty of the scene before us. Stretching ahead, as far as the eye could see, was lush green countryside spread out below us – the valley of the Irrawaddy.

Directly opposite, on the far bank of the river, arose a multitude of pagodas, glittering and glistening in the rays of the sun. Of every size and colour, they raised their slender towers to the brilliant blue sky and one could almost hear the tinkling of temple bells. This was Pagan, the ancient capital of Burma, which flourished in splendour long before the Romans conquered Britain.

After the monotony of the march, with one's view restricted to the sides of the track underfoot and often merely to the heels of the man in front, this view of space and colour, of background of temples and foreground of wide, fast-flowing river was more than a tonic. It was the goal terminating 450 miles of toil and labour.

By mutual consent we stopped the jeep at the side of the road and sat gazing in silence before us. Although we were still a mile or two away from the river itself it seemed, in that clear air, that we might almost lean forward and touch it. No sound reached our ears and the whole scene took on the aspect of a painting in a gallery – beautiful, but distant and hardly real.

Suddenly it dawned on us that the whole countryside beyond that water swarmed with the Japanese, and the spell was broken for ever. We were gazing not on the palaces of the kings of Burma but on the temporary home of the Japanese Army and, as far as we knew, we ourselves might already at this moment be under scrutiny through powerful binoculars. We started up the engine again and drove slowly and carefully forward so as to raise no telltale cloud of dust.

That evening the whole of the battalion was in occupation of the village of Myitche on the banks of the Irrawaddy and we slept that night under the stars in the cultivated gardens of a Poynggi Kyaung or Burmese monastery.

Thus ended the first phase of our advance against the Japanese which is described in the official history of the Burma Campaign as the master stroke of strategy on the part of General Slim. Our Phantom Force, moving through the hills with wireless silence, like so many green shadows flitting through the trees and along the trails, had now established itself at the edge of this mighty river and was already poised for the grand assault.

We wasted no time.

At this point the width of the Irrawaddy is 2,500 yards, nearly $1\frac{1}{2}$ miles; it is very treacherous indeed, with shifting sandbanks. Next day reconnaissances were carried out in preparation for the crossing.

A little bit of background concerning General Slim's strategy and intentions is essential to understand exactly why we were now committed to this dangerous venture.

The battle for Mandalay, 100 miles to the north of us, was mounting in ferocity and the eyes of the Japanese, and indeed of the world, were fixed on the City of Kings. The Japanese had rushed up maximum reinforcements through the town of Meiktila which was a nodal point lying south of Mandalay and eighty-five miles ahead of us, should we succeed in crossing the river. Meiktila was the main Japanese base and communications centre whose importance could not be underestimated. If Meiktila could be captured, then the Japanese army would be split into two parts, but the risks were great. Of the forces at his command General Slim had already committed three divisions to the fight for Mandalay, with two held in reserve which he had motorised or made airborne.

They were being held on leash to strike the mortal blow at the Japanese rear. But first our division had to force the crossing of the water at all costs.

The actual assault was to be made by the South Lancashire Regiment. The plan was for them to use assault boats powered by outboard motors and it was clever and detailed. They were to enter the water some miles upstream under cover of night and drift silently down with the current until opposite the selected spot. Then, at first light, the motors would start up and carry them surging across the river and onto the beach at the other side where there was a small hamlet marked on the map as Nyaungu. Support for the operation would be provided by concentrated fire from our side, on the west bank.

The essence of success was surprise. My company was detailed by the Colonel to act as carrier parties. Their task was to unload the boats from lorries, carry them no less than 600 yards across soft sand and place them in the water – all in the dark and with utter silence imposed.

During the day, we infiltrated in small parties to a plantation of palm trees some distance from Myitche so as to attract the minimum of attention, either from Jap eyes across the river or Burmese eyes about us. This little operation was carried out with studied casualness but, as soon as dark fell, we were galvanized into action and moved off as a complete company across country to the assault area. We cut across ploughed fields and paddy fields, through patches of cultivated crops and skirted plantations until we arrived at the rendezvous in good time but somewhat short of breath.

I was filled with admiration at the preparations which had already been made. The lorries, loaded with the boats, had halted some half a mile from the water's edge for secrecy. White tapes were laid out on the ground in clearly defined lanes, pinpointing the route to the river. At intervals, small red lamps glowed, secure in their hooded shields which rendered them visible only to our troops and invisible to the Japanese across the water.

Our immediate task was to unload the collapsible boats which were stacked on the vehicles, open them, secure them and carry them across that vital 600 yards to be placed silently on the water in readiness. A task indeed it proved to be. A boat that can be turned and manoeuvred easily in the water by the flick of a paddle or a turn of a wrist is a dead weight and an awkward bulk when out of its natural environment. I found it necessary to detail fifteen little Gurkhas to carry each boat. The sand was so soft that the weight of the carry drove those men down into it and up almost to their knees; each party had to pause every ten yards from sheer exhaustion. The strangled grunts forced from their throats bore testimony to the tremendous efforts put forth.

For hour after hour the work went on in the inky blackness until the last boat was bobbing gently up and down alongside its neighbours.

It was now 0300 hours and our job was finished. The men from the South Lancs were not due to embark in the boats for some time yet so I gathered my exhausted Gurkhas together and, with whispered wishes of good luck to the North Countrymen, we set out back over the fields to the zone of the impending battle.

This battle was obviously going to commence at dawn. Time was vital, so we hurried along at a cracking pace. About 0400 hours we reached our destination and flung ourselves on the ground in our exhaustion to try and snatch some sleep.

I put my haversack under my head as a pillow and no sooner had I closed my eyes, so it seemed, than I opened them again in the first faint mists of dawn. It must have been premonition. I sat up quickly and looked around at the sprawled figures, some stirring and aroused perhaps by the same feeling which had penetrated my sleep. At that very moment came the ugly rattling of machine gun fire in long bursts and bullets started whining their way over our heads. Sleep fled, and in its place butterflies took possession of our stomachs; fully awakened now, we crawled forward to observe the assault.

As the light grew, a fantastic sight lay before us.

The broad river surface was dotted with craft and the farthest boats were just touching down on the far bank and disgorging their tiny figures. The numbers who had succeeded in reaching their objective, however, were pitifully small. The remainder were under a hail of fire in the middle of the river and we could plainly see casualties mounting in boat after boat which had been hit. To add to the resulting confusion, the outboard motors on half the craft had proved unequal to the strain of their journey in lorries from India and had petered out. These boats were now drifting helplessly, spinning around and around in the swift current, some to stick fast on sandbanks as stationary targets; others to drift down the river, borne by the whirling waters out of sight of our straining eyes and straight into the hands of the Japanese.

A sense of horror gripped me as those lads, with whom we had laughed and joked a few hours previously, continued to drop under the hail of bullets. The drifting craft, draped with the bodies of the dead, trailing their lifeless limbs in the fuming currents, presented an awesome sight as the cries of the wounded carried to our ears across the water.

Those boats which had stuck in the sandbanks were the scenes of frantic activity as their crews tried vainly to push them off, with the bullets spurting into the sand around them.

We, on our part, were not idle on the west bank. Supporting fire was directed in great volume against the enemy positions which were cunningly dug into the face of the cliffs opposite us, overhanging the river. With a tremendous river like the Irrawaddy everything is in proportion. In some places on that river the banks tower above the water like the cliffs at Dover; and so it was here.

The Japanese gun emplacements had been dug out from the rear of those cliffs and they had also reinforced with concrete small caves which pitted the smooth face. To counter their advantage our tanks were brought up and lined our bank to be used as mobile artillery. The noise became deafening as they fairly plastered the Jap positions and also for good measure some buildings which were in view across the river. A great cheer went up as a direct hit was scored on a tall chimney which might have belonged to a factory or small power station and it came crashing down, first almost in slow motion and then in a spectacular burst of falling masonry and clouds of dust.

To our anxious and critical eyes, however, it was clear that the assault was a failure and we were beginning to wonder how many might survive the disaster. Those few who had gained a footing on the other side had climbed the cliffs in one part and could be seen through our binoculars moving about on the skyline. They appeared to be in company strength and, strange to relate, were never counter-attacked. It may be that the opposition realised the power of the forces which we were massing on our part and decided merely to delay us, but that company certainly survived. On the other hand, they may have gained their footing before dawn gave place to daylight and thus remained undiscovered for the time being.

Orders were now given to recall the boats and the remaining craft, as word got through, turned about and headed for our side. I was down at the water's edge to greet some of the survivors. Life in the ranks was tough indeed, especially on active service, and these men had been let down through no fault of their own. Their language was awful; they swore slowly, deliberately and without repetition and I felt a surge of pity as I heard them. They had seen their friends, their chums and their mates struck down at their sides, topple over into the bloody frothing water to vanish for ever; or drift in anguish straight into Japanese territory, without hope of pity should they survive the water and the bullets.

We received them with compassion and helped them ashore to where their battalion was endeavouring to rally its ranks of survivors, so small in number.

After this catastrophe an Indian battalion was given the task of crossing in broad daylight in full face of the opposition, as it was now essential to make a bridgehead without further delay. Every hour lost might mean that the Japanese could bring up powerful reinforcements and render still more difficult our thrust at their vitals. Our element of surprise was now lost and a straight fight lay ahead.

Those Indian sepoys made a magnificent job of it. They crossed the water in their little boats and leaped ashore with fixed bayonets to drive and hustle the enemy infantry clean off the river bank. A small foothold was gained and at once other troops started crossing to support their efforts. In a sense, the breaching of this mighty river was like the breaching of a dyke. On the one hand the veriest trickle of water, filtering through the solid dyke wall, soon swells to a flood which carries all before it. Here, the obstacle was water itself and the breaching agent a handful of gallant men whose numbers swelled in volume as the day wore on. By nightfall, sufficient forces were ashore to secure the bridgehead against Japanese reaction and counter-attack.

During all this time our whole battalion which was in reserve had been frantically busy assembling and launching rafts and barges, also constructing loading ramps for tanks and carrying out scores of unromantic but vitally important jobs; all without rest.

I could not help pondering that when Gurkha get down to work like this they are in their element and take some beating. All day they scurried about in orderly confusion, sparing no efforts and above all presenting cheerful faces to every situation which arose.

On 14th February 1945 the battalion crossed the river, thankful indeed to be finished with these tasks, but my company had to stay for one more day before joining them. I reflected ruefully that this day was St Valentine's Day – my own 29th birthday – and I could not imagine a more incongruous setting in which to celebrate it.

Next day the first prisoners were sent back across the river and I went forward to see them landing. To my astonishment, they were not Japanese at all but Indians who belonged to the notorious Indian National Army, fighting on the side of the Japanese. I felt livid with anger when I saw them. They knew perfectly well that they would be treated with scrupulous regard for the Geneva Convention or for the so-called rules of warfare, that they would not have to face torture or starvation; they were laughing and joking, very pleased with themselves. As they were loaded into lorries and driven away, grinning and chattering, I saw in my mind's eye the jeeps returning yesterday from this very spot, loaded with the stiff corpses of the gallant men of the South Lancs who had perished. I felt sick at heart and filled with a bitter hatred.

There is a corollary to all this. When the war was over and the citizen army had dispersed to its villages, I am grieved to report that in many instances these same traitors stalked about unharmed, boasting not only of their deeds but also of their atrocities, whilst many a brave and crippled sepoy found himself spurned and near to starvation. Congress triumphed and India gained her so-called freedom from the British Raj, but in the bloodbath which followed, as Indian slew Indian, how many thousands must have cried out for the days of the old Indian Army when, under British officers, Muslim, Hindu and Sikh united to drive out the Japanese army which would have laid waste every village and town on that continent.

India was once the brightest jewel in the Imperial Crown, but it is quickly forgotten that it was men of flesh and blood whose efforts kept it polished.

CHAPTER SIX

The Plain

The following day I myself stepped ashore with my company on the far bank and rejoined the battalion.

The troops at the actual bridgehead had received a visit from Lord Louis Mountbatten, the Supremo, who came across the river in a DUKW – a rather more sophisticated vessel than the canvas and metal contraptions to which we had entrusted our own precious bodies. It was a fleeting visit which I was sorry to miss. His presence, naval smart in his crisp white uniform, served to emphasize to us the importance attached in high places to our efforts. Those working at the beach, including our own Peter Myers, who was Beachmaster, were grimy and unshaven after their recent task. They felt rather dazzled by this naval occasion but no doubt their morale received a fillip. Peter loved to tell the tale, years afterwards, of the British sergeant-major standing nearby when the Supremo set foot on the shore. He obviously felt that the occasion called for something special. Raising his battered bush hat from his sweating brow, he called for three cheers for the Supremo: 'Hip - Hip - Hip -'. It was a very ragged 'Hurrah' which was croaked out from the throats of the assembled troops.

I sought out the Colonel and reported the safe crossing of my own company. He took me to the perimeter of the defences which had been thrown around the beachhead and allocated to me an area where we bivouaced. We were all keyed up with excitement now that the river lay at our backs, with the enemy in front. The foremost thought in our minds was: 'What is our next objective?'.

At this particular stage there were troops of the 33rd Indian Infantry Brigade ahead of us – the men who had actually breached the river. We were therefore able to investigate Pagan and found it to be a really fascinating town. There were plenty of brick-built houses, an unusual sight to our jungle eyes. There was also the usual conglomeration of shops and hovels that constitute the bazaar in any Indian or Burmese town. Most of the shops had their shutters up and no wonder, as the place bore plenty of evidence of the fighting in the shape of scarred or shattered masonry.

It was the pagodas and the temples, however, that held our eyes. On all sides they rose above us and the impression one gained was that of a mediaeval city, as indeed this was. I was informed long afterwards that there were some 300 temples in that holy place.

The largest pagoda was a sight not easily to be forgotten. Surrounded by countless smaller spires, the main temple blossomed like some gigantic lotus bud out of its beautiful setting of exquisitely carved, centuries-old moulding. The brickwork was composed of tier upon tier of concentric carving, each layer of a different pattern, and the whole tapering, ever more slender, as it rose higher. Surmounting the stonework was a glittering, shimmering pinnacle covered in gold and capped by a delicate crown of tinkling bells, ever gently sounding to any breeze that passed overhead.

The approach to the temple was up a wide staircase consisting of hundreds of steps flanked by wooden pillars. It was covered by an ornately carved wooden canopy which covered the pillars throughout their length. On climbing these steps I was quite surprised to find that the immediate environs of the pagoda housed a full-scale market. I could not help thinking at once of the moneylenders in the Temple.

As a group of us was leaving the temple we received another confirmation of the importance attached to our activities at the Irrawaddy when we beheld a film crew, complete with cameras and all the usual paraphernalia busily photographing us as we descended the stairway. Next time I wrote home I urged my mother to keep a sharp eye out for the Pathe Gazette News but she never saw the little episode.

We were not there, however, merely to admire the sights of Pagan. There was sterner business in hand and soon we were on our way.

The task of the division was to hold and to extend the bridgehead and our battalion received orders to pass through the holding troops and resume the advance to the south, moving parallel with the Irrawaddy.

At this time our brigade was responsible for a large slice of the countryside extending inland some miles from the river. Day by day we edged forward with caution, expecting to establish contact with the Japanese at any moment. The 1/11th Sikh Regiment and the King's Own Scottish Borderers were, of course, our neighbours and we all worked in close co-operation.

This part of Burma was utterly different from the country which we had previously traversed. Having crossed the great natural barrier of the Irrawaddy, we had now reached the Central Burmese Plain, the 'Purple Plain' so vividly described by the author H.E.Bates in his moving book of that title. The heat was relentless from early morning to dusk; the road which formed the main axis of our advance was a white ribbon, ankle deep in dust. Between villages the parched fields were divided one from the other by cactus hedges, several feet high and virtually impenetrable in depth. The whole scene shimmered in a permanent heat haze which strained the eyes and sometimes rendered one quite giddy.

As we marched onward our lungs became like fiery bellows, drawing in the hot air in panting gasps and expelling it in even hotter blasts whilst the ever present sweat traced channels down our dust-caked faces. Our pounding feet stirred up clouds of the dust and when our jeeps passed to and fro they left behind them tell-tale spirals in the motionless air – perfect targets for Japanese artillery.

At first we moved reasonably close to the Irrawaddy itself and it was heaven indeed, in the evening, to seek out the river and to plunge into its cool embrace. Fatigue seemed to dissolve on these occasions almost as if the waters possessed magical healing qualities. The oases of palm trees scattered along the banks made wonderful resting places and excellent bivouacs.

After a few days, however, our battalion was switched to the inland flank of the brigade, miles away from the blessed river, as protection against sudden attack. The Jap commanders were always very fond of the right or left hook. Here, the country was even more arid and was more like the Western Desert in North

Africa than Burma. As far as the eye could see, the plain rolled away inland, splashed here and there by green patches of villages – a depressing sight. The cacti seemed to grow ever larger and spikier and provided really nasty obstacles in many places.

Access to water became an urgent problem and we were always on the look-out for wells. Our tactical dispositions were to a great degree governed by this need and often our few jeeps had to make journeys of several miles to replenish our waterbottles, chaghals and water carriers carried on the mules.

One morning I was sitting at the summit of a small hill which rose out of the surrounding plain. It was just after the dawn Stand-to. As the sun rose higher in the sky and the heat started to bite, I became aware of movement away over to my left on the floor of the plain beneath us. Alert for signs of the expected Japanese attack, I whipped my binoculars to my eyes. My brain registered the fact that the tremendous scale of the movement was aimed towards the Japanese rather than coming from them and after scrutinising the scene carefully I gasped with astonishment. The whole onward impetus of the movement was mechanised. Vehicle after vehicle, jeep after jeep, lorry after lorry and tank after tank went surging across the flat plain in a steady, never-ending stream. We had not seen vehicles in numbers like this since the campaign had started and I was fascinated. With our few jeeps and mules, we were indeed the poor relations of this impressive armada, sailing across the plain in the gathering heat haze. They were heading due east in the direction of Meiktila which we knew was the key to the whole of the communication system of Burma – road, rail and airfield.

Little could I guess at the time, but I was then witnessing what the history books now refer to as the master-stroke of the Burma Campaign. It did however dawn on me why so much importance had been attached in those high places to the success of our fight for the Irrawaddy bridgehead. We had presented General Slim with the chance for which he had yearned – the opportunity to launch those armoured brigades against Meiktila to cut the Japanese in two. I was now seeing the start of the launching of the famous 17th Indian Division (The Black Cats) who had already covered themselves in glory earlier in the campaign before being taken out, ostensibly to rest, but in reality to train for this event. They crashed across that plain and covered the eighty-five miles in as many hours, not days.

Frank Owen, in his book *The Campaign in Burma,** describes this epic which paralysed the Japanese nerve-centre:

> Not that the enemy accepted his fate. He rushed up all the artillery he could muster to recover the lost nerve-centre of his army. Troops moving towards Mandalay were put in reverse, and even some already engaging XXXIII Corps were pulled out. Time and again Major-General Kasuya, the energetic commander at Meiktila, flung in his picked infantry, heavily armed with automatic weapons, to regain the airfields; to hold the town he ordered every hospital patient who could fire a rifle to fight until killed. They faithfully obeyed his order. The British and Indian infantry shot, bombed, burned and hacked their way into the strong-posts and barricaded alleys; the remainder of the garrison crouched in the cellars, and still fought. They were bayoneted to the last man. Whatever else they were, these Japanese earned Slim's hard tribute as 'the most formidable fighting insects on earth.'

General Kimura commanded the Japanese troops who now faced us. Up to the present we had not come face to face with the Japanese although we had been rudely awakened one night by prolonged firing, accompanied by shouts and cries when the Sikhs drove off an attack on their positions. The noise of the battle drifting over to us on the still night air sounded as if it were taking place right on top of us. We stood-to and for a considerable time it was difficult to believe that the whole action was a mile or so away. Meantime, word had reached us that a large patrol of the King's Own Scottish Borderers had walked into a Jap ambush and had lost many men. I later spoke to a soldier who was on the scene shortly afterwards and he described vividly the sight of the British bodies lying sprawled all over the track and on the verges. It was a sad lesson in fieldcraft.

Soon after this, our own battalion was blooded.

* Published by Arrow Books, 1957.

CHAPTER SEVEN

Gurkha Patrols

There was a village named Kinka close by the Irrawaddy and it was believed that the Japs occupied it in some strength. This village was on the opposite flank of the brigade. The Brigadier clearly had considered that a patrol from our battalion, operating right across the front of the brigade from our situation far inland stood a good chance of success through initial surprise; in fact, this would be to take a leaf out of the Japanese book.

The Colonel ordered a strong fighting patrol of a platoon, with a section of pioneers, to set out under command of Lieutenant Robert Findlay. They were determined to secure information and were prepared to fight for it. Our anxious thoughts went with them as they moved out into the dark.

It was the night of 25/26th February and after the moon rose the whole countryside was bathed in bright moonlight. It hung, immense in the dark velvet sky, the big perfectly round Burma moon, as we all watched them pick their way across the landscape until they dwindled in size and merged into the distance. For hours we waited anxiously, not sleeping. It was as if some part of ourselves was out there with them and our innermost thoughts travelled every part of the way with them.

It was past midnight when the distant crackle of small arms fire and the crump of grenades exploding came to our ears out of the silent night and brought us to our feet. The exchanges were vicious and prolonged and then stopped as suddenly as they had begun. I felt the muscles in my stomach tighten.

It was clear to us that we would not have any news for a few hours so we settled down to wait in an agony of suspense. What had they found? How many? Whose firing had we heard? What casualties? All these questions were foremost in our minds and had to remain unanswered at present.

The moonlight faded into darkness before dawn and gradually the darkness gave place to rosy streaks across the sky in the east. We stood-to as usual and as we still gazed out in the direction of Kinka the first few figures emerged out of the dawn mists.

There was no mistaking the jaunty stride of the Gurkha. Towards us they came, in twos and threes, their rifles across their shoulders, butt up and grasped by the stock – their favourite method of carrying when on active service.

Some were wounded and supported by their comrades but, as we counted them in, there did not seem to be any missing. It was with relief that we spotted the tall figure of Bob Findlay moving in their midst but we were sorry to see that one of his arms was shattered and tied up in an improvised sling. His face was deathly white, due partly to loss of blood and partly to exhaustion. We were so glad to see him and gave him a great welcome before hurrying him off to the doctor and the Colonel.

Of the success of the patrol there could be no doubt. They had found the Japs, accurately pinpointed their positions and he had attacked them at once. Eleven enemy dead were killed outright for the loss of five Gurkhas wounded, in addition to Bob Findlay. No less than seven of the Japanese dead fell before Havildar Gambirsing Gurung who was awarded an Immediate Military Medal for his exploit.

This was very definitely first blood to our battalion in this phase of the campaign and from then on our tails were up. During the next few months we were to take part in many savage encounters with the Japanese but we always had supreme confidence in our own ability to smash them. This attitude was so different to the early days of the Burma Campaign when the Jap appeared to be some form of Superman.

One amusing incident came to light in connection with this patrol.

Amongst our weapons we possessed a fairly new bomb – the M9A1 grenade. This consisted of a streamlined bomb, with long slender tail and was fired from a specially adapted rifle carried by the 'M9A1 Grenadier'. This weapon was fired horizontally, close to the ground, and was designed for use against Japanese bunker positions, with their narrow weapon slits. The idea was to aim at the slit in the bunker and to skim the bomb at it rather on the principle of the pebble skimmed across a pond. Even a near-miss produced results, as the construction of the bomb ensured that all blast effect was forward in direction, right in the faces of the bunker crew.

Up to now we had not had an opportunity of putting this weapon to the test in action but we expected great things from it and a 'Grenadier' was operating with the patrol. Later, when we captured Kinka, a very close examination, and an impromptu 'post-mortem', was made of the positions which had been attacked by the patrol. One of the bunkers was cunningly sited at the corner of a Pagoda and had collapsed under the onslaught. Just by it, however, flattened against the wall of the Pagoda, lay three M9A1 grenades, crushed flat by impact, but unexploded. The little man in his excitement had forgotten to remove the safety pins! His comrades had gathered round to congratulate him, but I walked away as the platoon Jemadar's congratulations turned to abuse. Truly, in the army you cannot win!

Shortly after this incident the battalion was switched back to the Irrawaddy side of the brigade and henceforth advanced parallel with, and fairly close to, the river.

When I say advanced, I must qualify this statement. The task of the brigade was not primarily to advance and capture ground at this time. We were still the 'beachhead' troops whose job it was to enlarge and hold that bridgehead. The fact that we had come a long way since crossing the river was irrelevant. Insofar as it fitted in with the Brigade and Divisional plans we were allowed to advance but permission had to be sought and also granted on each occasion.

This overall plan was strictly adhered to and later on we took part in 'killing operations' where we were permitted to advance, seize a village, kill Japanese and then retire to our own positions. In practice this had the immediate effect of luring the Japs back again to occupy the village until they were wiped out by further sallies on our part. This fitted naturally into the slogan given by General Slim: 'Destroy the Japanese Army where you find them.'

Patrolling was the order of the day. Each day small patrols were sent out to the south-east and the south-west, probing the ground

Major Denis Sheil-Small MC, taken in India in 1945.

Preparing to cross the Irrawaddy – February 1945.

in front of us for information about the enemy. This method was very thorough but proved rather slow for our Colonel who displayed at all times an aggressive determination to come to grips with the Japanese. He bent his mind towards the problem of how to hurry things up and came up with a solution – jeep patrols.

The jeep patrol consisted of two jeeps working together and containing an officer and six men divided between the two vehicles. The object was to press on down the road from one village to another, halting a few hundred yards short of the village. The jeeps would then be turned around ready for a quick get-away, if necessary.

The patrol would then proceed on foot and carefully comb the village for signs of Japs. If they met nothing in the way of opposition the jeeps were whistled up and they passed on to the next village, where the plan would be repeated.

This method was quick and produced results but it was hair-raising for the participants. It will be remembered that this countryside was open in character and the roads ankle deep in thick white dust. Any vehicle, therefore, travelling along them created its own spiral of dust which would hang in the air over it like some gigantic question mark. It was indeed an uncomfortable feeling to sit in such a vehicle and await events.

Soon the inevitable happened.

Our American, Scott Gilmore, was sent off one day with his small party of Gurkhas and they were ambushed after they had left the vehicle at the approaches to a village and were creeping forward on foot.

Now the reason the jeeps were turned about on those occasions for the quick get-away was not so much to succour the patrol as to save the vehicles. It is a grim and ironic comment on the values prevalent in war to consider that these jeeps were of more value almost than human life. Replacements were out of the question and the battalion depended on them to move the heavy stores, and to water and ration the companies. The drivers were therefore under strict orders to go and go fast at the first burst of firing. On this occasion they did so and came hurtling into the battalion perimeter with their story.

The patrol, meanwhile, had split up in accordance with their training and were making their way back by various tracks. They had their information – the village was in the hands of the Japs. Later that day Scottie came in safely, with the riflemen all accounted for. Subadar Kharakbahdur Gurung, a fine Gurkha Officer, was missing.

The story of this brave man is worth telling.

His experience of warfare had commenced on the far-off North-West Frontier of India against the Pathans, in so-called peace-time. At that time the Indian Army was holding those turbulent tribes in check, a thankless task carried out with extreme efficiency and no small display of gallantry on numerous occasions. Kipling knew it, and so does every old soldier who ever voyaged east of Suez in those bygone days when the sun was reputed never to set on the British Empire.

As a soldier, Kharakbahadur was first class and as an individual completely without fear. The news that he was missing was a bad shock to us and we prepared to mourn his loss. Next day, however, one of our out-posts gave a shout and pointed excitedly across country to where a diminutive figure was trudging across the open ground.

I got my binoculars focussed on to the figure and recognised Kharakbahadur at once. A second or two later I nearly dropped them in surprise as I made out what he was carrying. In addition to his tommy gun, which was slung over his right shoulder, he had a long-barrelled Japanese rifle slung over his left shoulder; clasped to his chest was a human head. I could clearly see the black hair and the Japanese features. As he came into focus of the eyes of the men about me they gave a tremendous shout and rushed forward to greet him and to escort him in.

His story was told in simple, stark language. When the patrol was ambushed he went to ground in a patch of jungle on the edge of the village. He hid there for the rest of the day. When night fell he emerged and made himself known to the Burmese villagers who were not too keen to have him in their midst. Obviously they were terrified of the Japanese reprisals.

Kharakbahadur found it necessary to threaten them with his tommy gun and they reluctantly gave him food and shelter for the night. He must have spent a very uncomfortable vigil, surrounded by reluctant allies. Clearly he could not afford to sleep or relax. Next morning he left them at dawn and set out to find his way back to us.

'I was travelling along a track,' he said, 'when I suddenly saw a Japanese patrol approaching. It seemed to me that the leading scout was rather far ahead of the main body so I lay in wait for him. As he passed by I grabbed him, dragged him into the jungle, chopped his head off with my kukri and seized his rifle. I slipped away before the main patrol had reached the spot.' As I listened to him the story put me in mind of a strike by a king cobra – fast, sure and deadly.

To most people this will have seemed a barbarous act, but none will deny the courage which he displayed. To up and kill in the face of an approaching patrol, hopelessly outnumbered and on the run, when he could well have lain doggo is surely proof of the courage which every commander prays to find in his men. To bring back the head was logical to his simple mind. How, otherwise, could he prove his little adventure?

I am sorry to say that after participating with gallantry in subsequent fighting this brave man met his death in Java in fierce hand-to-hand fighting.

There is a very human touch to the final scene in Scott Gilmore's patrol.

When he came in he reported at once to the Colonel who was anxious to pinpoint the place of ambush. The latest set of aerial photographs of the vicinity were laid out on the ground outside the CO's dugout; the CO himself studied them intently and plied Scottie with incisive questions. The latter, tired and weary, looking rather like some Gary Cooper, draped his six foot length over the photos and looked at them with a puzzled expression.

'Was it here?' said the CO, pointing.

'No, Colonel.'

'Was it here?' the Colonel's finger moved a fraction.

'I guess not.'

'Could this be the place?' pointing to a track junction.

There just seemed no way in which Scottie could pinpoint the exact spot at which he and his men had nearly died. Just as Colonel Walker was becoming really exasperated, Scottie's tired face broke into a charming smile. With utter candour he said: 'I know, Colonel, let's ask the Burma Intelligence Corps Corporal; he's a swell guy; he's sure to know.'

I will draw a veil over what Colonel Walter Walker said in reply to Captain Scott Gilmore.

Shortly after this episode the Colonel sent for me and outlined an ambitious plan which would take us into contact with the Japs sooner or later. He proposed that I should take my whole company, less one platoon, together with an artillery observation party and signals personnel and set out on a three days' patrol ahead of the battalion; the implication was that we needn't bother to come back until we had found the Japs.

The idea was to press forward, pick a suitable place for a patrol base, form a base and then patrol forward of that again; this was to be repeated until we bumped the Japs. We were equipped with wireless sets for communication.

Next morning we set off, some eighty strong, and headed south, moving astride the road in battle formation with the OP party in our midst.

The countryside was rolling, in gentle slopes, with the inevitable cactus hedges scattered about on either side. Each fold of ground was carefully scrutinized before we advanced to the crest of the next slope.

After covering some three miles in this fashion I found a spot which I considered to be suitable for a base. It was to the right of the road and well away from it, in close proximity to a chaung (dried up river bed). We offloaded the mules, sited our defensive positions and started to dig in. This took some little while and by the time that our foxholes had been carved out to the 'first task' the day was far spent.

I might explain that the 'first task' consisted of digging slit trenches to chest level. The pattern of trench digging was always the same. 'The first task', to be completed as soon as we arrived in a position where we would be likely to stay for a day, would provide protection against attack. 'The second task' meant deepening the trench to shoulder level and excavating sleeping accommodation under the forward lip. This would be carried out at a later opportunity. Finally, 'the third task' would mean adding the refinements – a firing step, elbow rests and cavities in which to place grenades, ready at hand for throwing.

Bunkers, in which the machine guns were sited, were rather more complicated and were always roofed over with tree trunks and earth and then camouflaged.

After, we took the evening meal. During this time I was contemplating our next move. It seemed to me that a night patrol would make good sense. Under cover of darkness it would cover the open ground without quite so much risk of discovery and carry on, as it were, the momentum of the original patrol. If the Japs were discovered then we would have achieved our object and if not, then the night would not have been wasted as we could close up the rear of the party and press forward next day.

Careful preparation was needed.

I decided to take the night patrol out myself and detailed one platoon – about thirty men – to accompany me. The remainder of the party were to be left as protection for the gunners and signals and to form a rallying point and rendezvous if we got into trouble. The need for detailed scheming and clear orders is paramount on these occasions. Those who are left behind must know when the patrol is going out, the routes it will take, when it is likely to return and, of course, the passwords.

There was no defined front in this campaign. Patrols on both sides roamed freely far behind the enemy rear for days at a time. Each little body of men provided themselves with all-round defence like a little island in an alien sea. If attacked, they would stand firm and give as good as they got. It was useless to retire. Where could they go?

By 2000 hours I left the patrol base and pushed forward with my platoon, to the accompaniment of whispered good wishes from the remainder.

To save time, we stuck to the road but advanced in leap-frog fashion. There were three sections; one would move by bounds to a distance of some 50/100 yards and then signal the all clear to the next one. They in turn would advance or 'leap' the first section and the third section would carry on the good work. Progress was not fast, but there is no other reasonable method of patrolling in the face of an enemy and in unknown territory.

I had observed from my map that some two miles ahead of us lay a largish chaung across our path, stone dry in this season, and I felt that this would make a natural halting place for us to take stock of our surroundings. It will be remembered that the Irrawaddy lay to our right and this was one of its countless tributaries in the wet season.

Some half a mile short of the chaung, however, we passed through a village consisting of a few typical Burmese houses on stilts, surrounded by cultivated plantations and palm trees. The houses were in darkness and the villagers wisely asleep inside. No villager in his right senses would wander abroad in Burma after dark at that time. We slowed down our pace to a crawl and crept forward step by step.

About halfway through the village a figure emerged from the shadows at the side of the road and made frantic but silent signals to us. I sent forward for the patrol to halt. Two Gurkhas detached themselves from the section and escorted the man over to where I had stopped under a tree.

The Burmese was clothed in a longgyi, with sandals on his feet. I was wondering how to address him as I did not speak Burmese. Before I could open my mouth, however, he spoke in English, clearly and faultlessly.

'The Japanese positions are not far ahead, Sir', he said, 'If you pass on down this road they will be sure to ambush you.'

The dispassionate calm with which he spoke, the perfect English which he used, the lack of surprise at seeing us all intrigued me immensely. The cultured tones he used were more suited to the atmosphere of a West End Club in London than to a dusty village in the heart of Burma; I was anxious to find out more about my informant.

Sensing my unspoken query, he went on:

'I was a Police Officer here before the war,' he said, 'When the Japanese came, they tortured me and murdered my family. I escaped and I have been living here for three years in the house of my brother-in-law. In the daytime I work as a coolie in the fields but I sleep in his house and my sister looks after me.'

As the Burman spoke I watched him carefully. Was he speaking the truth? Unfortunately, many people had already died through treachery on the part of a Burmese minority and in consequence all were suspect. His next words added to my dilemma.

'If you will be good enough to accompany me to the house,' he said, 'we shall be able to talk more freely. I have made notes of the Japanese forces and dispositions and I would like to give them to you.'

This was indeed tricky. Was he leading me straight into a trap or would my caution lose the opportunity to gain the information we were all searching for?

The moment called for a snap decision and I decided to take a chance.

I gave orders to my second-in-command, Subadar Jitbahadur Thapa, to allow the patrol to advance slowly to this side of the chaung and there to await my orders. On no account was he to cross the open sand. I then took one section with me and signalled for the Burman to lead the way.

We threaded our way along a narrow path between two small gardens until we came to the place. The house stood in its own compound and, like its neighbours, was raised off the ground on stilts. I posted my men around the compound and outside the house and with a sense of uneasiness followed our guide up the steps. At a signal from me, my orderly came with me.

The room which we now entered was the main living room of the house. It contained a bamboo table and some chairs; a bed stood in one corner. An oil lamp was burning on the table and illuminated the centre of the room, leaving the corners in shadow. A woman of middle age came forward to greet us and was introduced by the Police Inspector as his sister. She was of a pleasant disposition and quite good-looking.

After inviting us to seat ourselves at the table she departed from the room for a few moments and then returned with a plate of some Burmese sweetmeats, a jug of water and some glasses. I could not very well refuse this offer of hospitality and politely helped myself to one of the concoctions. My orderly had meantime positioned himself at the door and I noticed his keen glance summing up the situation.

Our host seated himself at the table and started to speak very earnestly:

'The next village up the road is named Milaungbya,' he said, 'and for many months the Japanese have been using it as a convalescent depot for their wounded. They have suffered terrible casualties fighting your troops up north and hundreds of wounded have passed through here. They have come in lorries, in bullock carts and on foot.'

I thought of the advance up north against Mandalay and the Irrawaddy crossings, and it was heartening to hear that we were taking such a heavy toll of the Japanese.

He went on: 'They have now evacuated their casualties from Milaungbya but they have positions dug in around the village. It is clear that they intend to fight you there.'

In answer to my further questions, the Burman stated that the village of Singu which was a few miles farther on was a most important Japanese base from which they were in the habit of crossing the river and supplying their troops on the western side. This was a vital piece of information since I already knew that these same troops were causing no end of delay to the East African Brigade who were operating in that area. The capture of Singu would do much to assist our friends across the river.

Every question which I asked received a quick and intelligent answer and my doubts about the man began to disperse. He explained a good deal about Singu. It was the last village guarding the approaches to the oilfields and the town of Chauk. It stood this side of a very wide chaung whose dry sandy bed extended several hundred yards across. It appeared that the Japanese had fortified it very strongly with permanent defences and it was undoubtedly a key position. Later events were to prove how truthfully that Police Inspector had spoken.

After giving me details of a red brick-built house which was the Japanese Headquarters for the district, he went on to outline the dug positions as far as he had observed them. By this time I was taking copious notes in my field service notebook; I also made a sketch map which I checked carefully with him.

Just as I rose to my feet and was thanking him for his help, the silence of the night outside was shattered by a vicious burst of machine gun fire. It was definitely Japanese. There could be no mistaking that rapid, flat-sounding crackle. It was firing in prolonged bursts and was joined by rifle fire and the thump of grenade explosions.

To my ears it sounded extremely close and I assumed that we were under attack. With one bound I jumped at the table and extinguished the oil lamp, half expecting the crash of bullets through the thin slatted bamboo walls. I headed towards the door where my orderly was urgently calling my name. As I prepared to dash down the steps, the Burman who had fallen on his knees in fright clasped my legs and hindered me.

'Don't go outside,' he cried, 'they will know I have been talking to you and they will kill me.'

There was no time for pity. I told him to shut up and dashed down into the compound. My section of Gurkhas were all at their posts, calmly awaiting orders. After a few moments I gathered them together and we made our way to the road, hoping to find out what was going on.

Just as we reached it the firing stopped, as suddenly as it had started, and utter silence fell about us. I expected to find the rest of the platoon there, but nobody was in sight. Slowly it dawned on me that in spite of my orders, Jitbahadur had taken them on up the road and they must have been ambushed at the chaung. The fact that the firing had ceased entirely puzzled me. Surely to God they had not all been wiped out? I decided to investigate and we crept slowly forward towards the chaung.

A few moments later, the sound of running feet came from directly in front of us and out of the darkness came the figure of Jitbahadur and a mere handful of men, not more than three or four. Even in the gloom I could see that his eyes were as large as saucers, set rigid by shock and wildly staring. He grasped my hands and blurted out his story in broken gasps.

He had obeyed my order to advance slowly as far as the chaung but somehow had misunderstood my instructions to halt this side until I had finished with the Burman. He led the platoon forward over the sandy floor of the chaung and halted in the middle whilst he decided to give orders to his section commanders to take up positions. It was dark but they must have been quite visible against the white sand. Immediately, the Jap machine guns had opened up at point-blank range from a distance of only a few yards and men had dropped to the ground everywhere. He crawled back to the bank on this side where he collected the few he found there and they had run back to give us warning.

As he gabbled on I realized that he was physically shocked and needed a violent antidote. I struck him hard across the face and shook him by the shoulders. The reaction was immediate. His eyes seemed to turn in on themselves and then came rapidly into normal focus and his voice lost its hysterical tone. He was still convinced that the remainder of the patrol had perished and the others nodded vigorously to confirm his view. Two of them added that they had seen figures moving around the flank which proved that the Japs were sending out a counter-patrol to cut us off.

I had been listening carefully for cries of wounded as it seemed incredible that everyone else had been killed; but no sound came from the chaung. Now I had to make my decision. Was I to return to the rendezvous at patrol base and leave the dead behind? We had achieved the object of the patrol; we had bumped the Japs; we had information about Milaungbya and Singu, together with details of the Jap defences and that information had to go back. We could do nothing for the dead and if we lingered much longer the flanking Japs would cut us off. Our total strength was reduced to about twelve.

I listened intently and went forward to a bump in the ground near the chaung and listened again; no sound came forth, so I gave the order to make for the rendezvous.

We travelled very fast over the few miles separating us and were heartily welcomed by those whom we had left at base. The sound of the firing had reached them across the night air and they were anxiously awaiting to hear our news. They had been standing-to for some time.

As we were relating our melancholy news, a sentry caught sight of a few shadowy figures approaching the position. We expected a Jap patrol and prepared to give them a hot welcome. As they came closer, however, the outline of Gurkha felt hats showed up clearly against the skyline and we held our fire. Gurkhas indeed they were

– from the chaung. As the night wore on, they turned up in twos and threes out of the shadows, survivors all. It seemed that no-one had been killed after all.

The Jap machine guns were high on the banks of the chaung, probably firing on fixed lines, and the bullets must have passed just above the heads of our men on the floor of the chaung. Everyone had dropped at once, instinctively, and in the confusion each thought that the others had died so, individually, they had crawled away to make for the rendezvous. Some had headed east and some west, to make detours and avoid a Jap follow-up.

Our rejoicing was immense, but poor old Subadar Jitbahadur could not look me in the face for days. He thought that he was in disgrace. If, however, anyone feels critical of him, I would invite them to walk into the muzzle of a Jap machine gun on a dark night and nearly have the top of their head blown off at point-blank range.

I lost no time in contacting the Colonel over the wireless and told him of our adventures. He was pleased that we had established contact with the Japs and told me to stay where I was. The idea in his mind was to bring up the rest of the battalion to join us but, first, he would have to obtain permission from high up in view of our role as the bridgehead troops. It was suggested that we should form a really strong position at our little base and patrol forward again to obtain further information as to the actual disposition of the Japanese force in Milaungbya.

Again it seemed to me that this called for another night patrol, so we spent the whole day in strengthening our defences and taking stock of our immediate surroundings.

When darkness came, I took a section of men under Subadar Kharakbahadur Gurung, he of the Jap head, and crept out of the position towards the Japanese. I wanted to effect complete surprise, so we made a very wide detour. The object was to move in a very wide semicircle and come in to the rear and flank of the Jap positions, hoping that they would be watching their front for any sign of activity on our part.

As I have said before, moving on patrol at night is a slow business. There is always the possibility of bumping into an enemy patrol, and in Burma the villages at night seem to be thronged with dogs. Given half a chance, they set up such a barking, yelping and snapping that your presence is revealed for miles around. Once they get wind of you and start up their chorus you may as well write off further patrolling around that particular village for the rest of the night.

We started off in darkness; after an hour or so the moon rose high and the whole scene was bathed in light. It was necessary to make use of every shadow in our stealthy advance, much of which lay along the edge of cactus hedges. About midnight, I was delighted to find the chaung right in front of us and I knew that my navigation had not led us astray. To the best of my calculations the Jap positions lay on the opposite side – over to our right. We halted awhile there to rest and gain strength for the tricky part which lay ahead. We had to cross the bed of the chaung and probe those positions for information. Crossing the white sand in moonlight presented the same problem as crossing a road. There are schools of thought. Some advocated infiltrating in ones or twos, but this popular method has one big disadvantage – if the first or second group is spotted by some alert sentry then the enemy will be waiting for the rest, with weapons ready sighted. If, however, you all go together in one silent rush it is always possible that you will either remain unseen or that a sentry will doubt his eyes if he detects the rapid movement; he may put the vision down to fatigue. After staring out from a slit trench for an hour or so at night, the very trees appear to walk about in front of tired eyes.

We chose the latter method, but took the precaution of posting our Bren gunner to give covering fire if anything went wrong. He was beautifully placed and would be firing in enfilade into the Jap positions.

The crossing was accomplished in seconds.

We were now well and truly on the flank of the enemy and were approaching them at right angles to their front. We narrowed the gap to about 100 yards and fortunately struck there a patch of broken ground which afforded excellent cover for movement.

At this stage the patrol's efforts became individual. The subadar, a naik (corporal) and two riflemen spread out and edged forward on their stomachs to observe; the remainder of us lay down and prepared to give them covering fire. Slowly they crawled forward

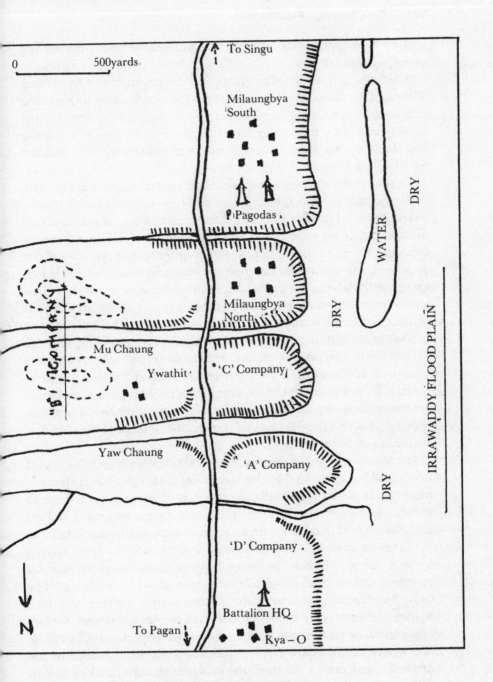

SKETCH OF MILAUNGBYA

and by now were some fifty yards from where we suspected the main position lay.

Suddenly, a Jap rose straight out of the ground in front of Naik Thamansing Bura, threw a grenade which burst with a deafening roar but fortunately missed the crawling figure, and then turned back to run. In a flash the naik let fly with his tommy gun and the Jap flung up his arms with a shriek and collapsed, clean riddled with bullets.

Pandemonium now broke loose. Over to the right a machine gun stuttered into life and the air above our heads crackled with bullets passing over. Jap rifle fire added to the din from immediately in front of us. It was clear that the Jap who had died had been an outpost in front of the main position in order to give warning of our approach. He must have been on his own and it was a suicide job. Once spotted, he stood little chance of regaining his comrades. This was not the only time we were to meet this sort of situation and it proved just how cheaply the Japanese commanders held life.

Two other instances come to my mind. In one case a Jap effort to destroy our supporting tanks consisted of a solitary soldier squatting in a shell hole in the road, in company with an aircraft bomb. His intention was to let a tank pass over his head and then to detonate the bomb at the moment of impact. Fortunately he was spotted by a sharp-eyed Gurkha moving to the flank of the tank and was shot before he could act.

On another occasion the plan was diabolically clever. The cactus hedges which abounded in the area presented a terrible obstacle to infantry as they were perfectly capable of tearing your flesh to shreds. As nature's barbed wire they were a huge success. The Japs in question had tied back with string or creepers sufficient branches of cactus on their side of a particular hedge to enable them to dig a foxhole, literally within the hedge. Two of them had then taken up positions inside with a machine gun and cut the string. The branches sprang back to their normal shape, leaving the Japs within and utterly invisible. To our eyes the hedge looked like any other. Advancing over the field, however, we were met with a hail of fire whose origin could not be traced. As we were pinned to the ground, our faces in the dirt, one of our tank commanders caught sight of my frantic signals, swerved his tank off his line of advance, and flattened the hedge and the Japs underneath it.

One ponders on the cold-blooded fanaticism of such troops and commanders alike: the one to accept certain death and the others to condemn them to it. Against such opposition it will be realised how immense was the task of the Fourteenth Army in Burma who had to destroy them or perish themselves. The issue was simplicity itself – destroy or perish. No more; no less. One can also appreciate how our hospitals behind the lines had to open special wards for unfortunate men whose minds gave way under the strain and the horror of it all; citizen soldiers who before the war had never seen even a motor accident and who now found themselves condemned to an existence in filthy holes in the ground, scorched by the sun or half-drowned in the monsoon rains and forced to witness the ever present sight of bloody mangled flesh and splintered bones, surrounded by the sweet stench of death.

In spite of the Jap fire, we did not fire back as our job was to observe and to get information. The sight of that machine gun, however, whose muzzle spurted flame, was too much for our Bren gunner. He suddenly opened up from behind us with two short bursts and was at once answered by further bursts from a second Jap gun on the opposite flank. There were now three machine guns fighting a triangular duel and our ears were drumming with the concussion.

I felt angry with our Gurkha for a minute for exposing his own position, but his action was a blessing in disguise. We had pinpointed two machine gun posts which indicated the strength of the opposition and our task was done. Also, I did not want us to be involved in a running fight which might last long enough to strand us in the open when dawn broke; a large part of the night had already passed. I gave the order to fire and we loosed off at the flashes whilst our observers crawled back to us. We then took advantage of our Bren gun fire to retreat swiftly to where the chaung turned a bend; there we recrossed and halted whilst our Bren gunner joined us.

We now set off quick for home and moved across country at a really cracking pace. A corner of my mind wondered whether the Light Infantry Brigade ever moved quite as fast as this under Wellington in the Peninsular War. I suppose my earlier days with the Rifle Brigade had prompted this strange thought. As we covered the ground we could still hear the Japs firing and they were now using rifle grenades. I presume they thought that our activity denoted an attack. We grinned as we pounded along.

The moon had set by now and it was not far off dawn when we arrived at the patrol base, breathless but triumphant. It is always a wonderful feeling to return to your lines after a brush with the enemy and our inner glow of satisfaction was enhanced by our reception. The British gunners in particular always have a soft spot in their hearts for 'Johnny Gurkha', as they call him, and they now clustered around, patting the smiling riflemen on their backs and handing around the cigarettes.

We stood-to at dawn; afterwards I informed the Colonel over the wireless of the gist of the night's work and he told me to report back in person to him without delay. As the patrol base was to remain in being, I handed over to my second-in-command and set off with my orderly for the battalion positions.

On passing through the outpost companies I reached Battalion HQ and found the Colonel in his command post. He was intensely interested in all I had to tell him and repeated that he was about to bring up the battalion to the patrol base and that undoubtedly we would launch an attack on the Japs in Milaungbya. As well as being interested in the details of Singu received from the Burman, the CO was particularly glad to know of the Jap machine gun posts which we had discovered. Knowledge of them should save lives in the coming full scale attack.

After offering congratulations which were to be passed on to all members of the patrol, Colonel Walker rather startled me with his next remark.

'I want you yourself to take a jeep at once and report to Brigade HQ. The Brigadier himself wishes to hear the story from your own lips. There's no need to wash or shave. Off you go, quickly.'

I felt very dirty and scruffy at this time as I had no time to refresh and smarten up; but I set off without further delay and reached Brigade later in the morning. The Brigadier was very charming and listened intently to my story; he inspected my notebook and the sketch of Singu with particular interest. He made detailed notes himself and then terminated the interview with his congratulations.

Gurkha crossing the Irrawaddy. In spite of his load (including 3″ mortar and Bren Gun —
by his right hand) he still remains cheerful.

(Left) Subadar-Major Chandru Thapa OBI, MC, 4/8th Gurkha Rifles, 1945. *(Right)* Jemadar Jitbahadur Thapa MC, after promotion to Subadar; MC won at Milaungbya with 'B' Coy, 5th March 1945.

Burma, 5th March 1945. Irrawaddy River near Ywathit, outside the Colonel's bunker. Bill Blenkin, Denis Sheil-Small, Pat Davis (4/8th Gurkha Rifles) after the 'MC' battle.

'Well done, Sheil-Small. You look as if you could do with a wash and brush up and I think that our rations will stretch to providing you with breakfast.'

I was then handed over to a Staff Captain who made the necessary arrangements. After a wash, shave and some bacon and eggs I felt a new man.

After visiting one or two old friends on the staff at Brigade I returned to the place where the battalion had been that morning only to find that they had all gone forward. In their place my own company was awaiting me, having been brought back into reserve for a rest. I now had visions of a few days of utter peace in quite a tranquil spot after the last few days of tension, exertion and violence.

The remainder of the day was indeed pleasant as we settled down in our fresh surroundings. The whole of the company took the opportunity of washing themselves and their clothing and of thoroughly cleaning their weapons. That night we all slept extremely well.

I had plans for recreation and games the next day, but those plans were not to materialize.

CHAPTER EIGHT

Fort

First thing next morning, I received an urgent message direct from the Colonel. He ordered me to bring my company forward again and to meet him at 0900 hours in the vicinity of the village where I had met the Burman in the night. I gathered that an attack had been carried out the previous day on Milaungbya by 'C' Company, under Peter Myers, and that it had been successful, although several men had been killed. The company was now busy consolidating its position at the spot to which we had penetrated on our night patrol. The CO, however, required our services once more, but did not tell me in what capacity.

I was disappointed that my men would not now enjoy their rest after all and I called for my Subadar to tell him. I also instructed him to have the company ready to move.

I must say that the Gurkha is nothing if not philosophical. Not a shadow of annoyance passed over his face. He looked me straight in the eyes, listened to my orders and at the end uttered the one word – 'Hos'. This is a Gurkhali word meaning, 'It will be'.

Within no time at all we had packed up, loaded the mules and were once again on the march up the road towards the battalion, blissfully unaware of what the immediate future held in store for us.

Even at this early hour the heat was beginning to grip the whole countryside and the steady crunch of our marching boots powdered the track beneath our feet. Clouds of dust, as fine as flour, assailed our nostrils and penetrated deep into our lungs. Many of us tied handkerchiefs around our faces but they did little to protect our lungs. We did not tarry on the march, but pressed steadily on until we came to the battalion headquarters. This was set off the road, to the right, in the vicinity of a large pagoda. The Colonel's command post had been dug out almost within its shadow. There was no time to admire either the slender spire or its tinkling bells; a guide was standing by the road to greet us and to escort me to the Colonel. I halted the company and they fell out for a rest; little did we realise that this would be the last rest for a very long time.

Colonel Walker greeted me pleasantly and explained what was in the wind. 'C' Company were now firmly dug in in front of Battalion HQ, after their attack the day before. However, the CO was anxious about the area to our left. This whole area consisted of uneven ground, patched by some villainous-looking cactus hedges. Between us and the line of 'C' Company there was a very wide and dry riverbed, or chaung, some fifty yards wide. Sprouting out of the glittering sand were clumps of tallish reeds or grass; the banks of the chaung and the environs consisted of barren, stony knife-edge ridges over which shimmered a heat haze.

The Colonel's appreciation of the situation was that the Japanese must be contemplating a counter-attack on 'C' Company which stood between them and the Battalion Headquarters; the whole left flank of the battalion was at present horribly exposed.

'I am sorry to call upon you again, Denis,' he said, 'but you can see for yourself where the danger to the battalion lies. If the Japs indulge in their usual flanking movement they can hit the soft under-belly of the battalion and wreak havoc amongst us. I want you and your company out there somewhere to the left. Your job will be to stop them at all costs.'

He then suggested that we take a platoon from my company and make a reconnaissance in force over the ground to choose a position from which my company might afford the greatest protection, not only to Battalion HQ but also to 'C' Company's flank.

As we cautiously crept forward over the ground, each undulation seemed to lead on to another so that we had to press quite far before finding a commanding position from which to view the countryside stretching before us. In this manner we finally reached the edge of the chaung itself. From here it could be seen that the ground on the opposide side fell away quite steeply. It was clear that this would be the ideal position for our purposes as a company of troops dug in at this spot would afford exactly the protection which the CO desired for the battalion.

We had our binoculars out and slowly swept the field of vision in front of us. We knew that the Japanese were there, but we could see no movement. The village of Milaungbya, with its stilted houses, bamboo bashas, cultivated gardens and tall palm trees, lay over to our right and in front of 'C' Company. It was from this village that the Japs had retreated yesterday in the face of 'C' Company's spirited attack. Our policy at this time was not necessarily to occupy villages; it was to bring the Japanese to battle and, in accordance with General Slim's Order of the Day, to destroy the Japanese army. We knew that by now they would have infiltrated back into the village.

We stayed for quite a while, searching our front, but still no sign of life did we see. Finally, the Colonel expressed the opinion that they might have retreated for a mile or so, or even right back to the next village – Singu. He suggested that my company should dig in here. A runner was sent back with orders to bring up my other two platoons. Colonel Walker also promised me that I would receive a detachment of 3″ mortars in addition to a further section of medium machine guns manned by the Frontier Force Rifles. Whilst these reinforcements were coming up, the CO stayed for a little while longer and discussed the general situation. Again he stressed the importance of holding the position at all costs.

Before he went back I was told to visit Battalion HQ for a conference that evening, after the usual stand-to. Meanwhile, the remainder of the company had arrived, together with the section of mortars and I was left free to site my platoons and the machine guns. I settled one platoon on the near bank of the chaung and led the other two across the sand. After choosing temporary positions for these platoons on the reverse slope of the steep, bare ground, I made a further reconnaissance with the jemadar who was in charge of the machine guns.

Together, we crawled forward over to the left of the position where a shallow spur jutted out forward of the ridge. This seemed to me to be an excellent place for a medium machine gun which could then fire in enfilade across our front should the Japs attempt to rush our position. We chose the site most carefully and then crawled back to issue the necessary orders.

Suddenly, without any warning, there came a violent explosion right in the middle of the chaung, followed by four or five more in rapid succession. In seconds the air was full of flying sand and clouds of acrid smoke. Mortar bombs were dropping amongst us. Simultaneously, the air above our heads began to hum with flying bullets as a Japanese machine gun opened up somewhere in front of us. It was soon joined by another; moments later a third gun stuttered into life. The noise was now deafening.

We slid and slithered our way down the stony incline into the chaung and then ducked and weaved through the explosions to see how the platoons were faring. The jemadar dashed across to the rear platoon where his machine guns were waiting; I joined the two forward platoons who had taken up firing positions in the only available place – manning the forward bank of the chaung. This stony ridge ran in a slight curve so that we were all disposed in an arc, which was to prove a blessing.

Everything happened at once.

In the first few minutes, just as I reached the men of my own company headquarters, my wireless set exploded after receiving a direct hit from a mortar bomb. My mind registered the fact that I was now completely out of touch with headquarters, an unfortunate start to my first battle. At the same time, Japanese figures could be seen running towards us, about a hundred yards away. A great shout went up from the Gurkhas and I then saw what was happening just in front of us. A section of riflemen had gone forward with the platoon commander, Jemadar Jitbahadur Ale, to a small rise some fifty yards ahead, from which vantage point he had no doubt been continuing his reconnaissance. They were now isolated and in the direct path of the attack. If the Japs worked around to the flank they would then be firing into the backs of our men.

I saw the jemadar jump to his feet, shouting encouragement to his men, and seize the bren gun. He waved them back by violent signals, ran forward himself and flung himself down on the ground to give covering fire. Without hesitation he engaged the Japanese machine and started a fierce duel with telling effect; moments later its incessant chatter faltered as his bursts found their target. By now, his men were a dozen or so yards to his rear and they turned to give him covering fire, in which we all joined. In this way, by fire and movement, the jemadar and his men regained our ranks without casualty.

To assist this section in their plight, I shouted to the havildar in charge of the 3″ mortars for rapid fire on the Japanese who were following up. He moved like lightning. His men had taken cover under the bank of the chaung because of the falling mortar bombs but he roused them into action. In no time a stream of our own missiles were curved high in the air to fall and burst with shattering effect amongst the Japs who faltered in their stride and went to ground.

It must be realised that at this time we had no positions of any sort dug in. The picks and shovels were still on the backs of the mules, so all we could do was to lie down on the bare, stony ground to fight back. Each of us took the best advantage he could of any little rock or dent in the soil which might afford cover, no matter how sparse.

Jemadar Jitbahadur joined me where I lay with his platoon, just under the crest of the ridge and it soon became clear that the attack was directed at this position. The Japs had now reached the little rise vacated by Jitbahadur and they had set up another machine gun on it. They had a clear view of our ridge and they concentrated their fire; stones, dirt, slivers of rock and ricocheting bullets flew about in all directions right in front of our faces. To add to our discomfort, we now became aware of a new sound.

A series of sharp, ear-splitting bangs denoted a shower of grenades falling upon us. They were being fired from the Jap rifle grenade dischargers and they were distinctly unpleasant. They were also the prelude to another rush by the enemy infantry.

As they came on, leaping and bounding over the ground, I heard for the first time that blood-curdling Japanese war-cry 'Banzai! Banzai!' We met them full and square with a hail of fire from all our weapons. Some of them died at once and the remainder were forced to ground again by the accuracy and intensity of our fire. At this point, as a Japanese officer was frantically trying to rally his men, Lance-Naik (Lance-Corporal) Krishnabahadur Ale who was in charge of the section amongst whom I was lying seized the section bren gun and leaped to his feet. Standing in full view of the

Japanese, on the crest of the ridge, he started firing from the hip. Burst after burst hammered from his gun as, all the time, he shouted a Gurkha war-cry. His very brave action soon drew the attention of the Jap machine gunners and the ground around his feet erupted into clouds of dirt and dust.

Suddenly Krishnabahadur dropped as if pole-axed. The bren gun fell from his numbed hands and came clattering back down the incline. As he lay there on the skyline, his head had fallen right back and his whole face was a mask of blood which rendered him unrecognisable. It did not seem possible that he could still be alive. The Gurkhas about me were shouting, 'Maryo! Maryo!' (He's dead! He's dead!) and, indeed, I too was convinced that he was dead. As the bullets continued to thud into the ground around him I felt revolted at the thought of his body being further mutilated. Crawling closer, I stretched out my hand to pull him down below the lip of the ridge.

Gurkhas are fatalists and his companions, assuming that he was dead, tried to restrain me by grabbing my ankles. I just managed to get one hand hooked into the collar of his battledress before they pulled me back to safety. As both of us came sliding back down, the bloody head moved slightly and I just caught the word '*Marynna*'. He was not dead! It was now the work only of a few seconds to ease him down amongst us. I then saw a frightful wound across his forehead, just above the eyes. This had turned back a flap of flesh, exposing the bone. Blood continued to pour down his face in a stream, staining my hands and saturating my bush shirt.

We laid him gently under a rock as protection against the sun and the grenades and applied a field dressing to his head. Just as I was binding it up, another great shout from the Gurkhas gave warning of a further rush by the Japs. Their yelling could easily be heard.

I jumped up and looked over the top to see that they were now much nearer and closing fast. I realised that a hand-to-hand fight was quite inevitable and I eased my kukri out of its scabbard, shouting to the others to do likewise. I also put four grenades on the ground handy for throwing. This move did not go unnoticed by the Gurkhas, who followed suit. This action appealed to them and they started to shout with glee.

By now the Japs were so close that we launched a volley of grenades at them and bent down to pick up more. Simultaneously, the air above us filled with a roar like an express train tearing through a station. It took my confused mind a few moments to realise that these were shells, our own shells, as was proved by the rapid thudding of our own artillery from far behind us.

Down came the shellfire right amongst the Japs. To my horror, the following salvo fell on my rear platoon position in bursts of flame and smoke. It appeared that the Colonel, hearing the uproar of our battle, and knowing that we had had no time to dig in sensed that we were about to be overrun; he made a snap decision – vital and dangerous – to fire off the map alone, without artillery observers. He knew that we were somewhere astride the chaung but he could not know where I had placed my platoons. It is decisions like this which win battles but not without cost.

The result was immediate, startling and impressive.

The Japs who had just rushed into our shower of grenades were suddenly enveloped by clouds of smoke as the shells found their targets; they were trapped by bursting shells in front and behind them. As more and more bodies started to fall they lost stomach for the fight. In five minutes the survivors had stumbled blindly back to their starting point at the village. They were hotly pursued by our own fire and the bursting shells.

A loud cheering broke out amongst the men around me, but I was speechless for the moment, with my eyes glued to my rear platoon. I could see figures lying still on the ground and others crawling painfully to shelter; it was only too obvious that we had suffered casualties from our own shells. There were both dead and wounded.

No blame must be attached to anyone. It was an episode of war, tragic but unavoidable and due to the peculiar accumulation of circumstances. Colonel Walker made his decision and it saved us. Although we lost men I am totally convinced that many of us owed our lives to the decision taken that day. The passing years have not changed my mind.

The Japanese attacking us had clearly been preparing for a counter-attack on 'C' Company but, seeing us about to occupy a vital feature, had switched that attack straight on to us. It was our misfortune that they were so well prepared. It was a rapid and clever appreciation of the situation on the part of the Japanese commander. We estimated that there were over 300 of the enemy and the ferocity of their attack needed some holding. For a number of my company, including myself, it was the first time in action and I was pleased to see how they stood their ground.

We now thought that we had a respite. Just as we were congratulating ourselves, the first Japanese shells fell upon us.

They had presumably arranged artillery support for their forthcoming attack on 'C' Company but now brought it down on us. As our positions were astride the chaung they had an easy target for identification from the map. The first shells sailed over our heads, falling behind my unfortunate rear platoon which had already suffering the tragic mishap. The remainder fell into the sand of the chaung and along its banks. The shooting was accurate, but by great good fortune no-one was killed.

The Japanese infantry were not long in following up but by this time our artillery had stopped firing, probably to seek out and engage the Japanese guns. The result was that we had to take the brunt of their rush with our own weapons. The engagement was fierce and short. As they broke again and turned to run our artillery fired again. Once more many of the Japs were caught in the open and dropped where they stood.

All this time I had no contact with the Colonel. I now selected a very intelligent young rifleman to run the gauntlet to Battalion HQ with a message. He was a youngster whose face I well remembered from the parade grounds in Quetta, where he was a recruit of great promise. I briefed him to tell the Colonel exactly where our position was, platoon by platoon, the strength of the enemy, the direction of their attack. I also asked for shellfire onto the village from which the attacks were being launched. There was no need to dwell on the Japanese shellfire as each bursting shell could be heard for miles around. Away sped the boy like an arrow, proud at his selection and determined in his task.

As I watched him go, I thought of the days and weeks spent on the drill square in Quetta, teaching him and his friends the elements of discipline and fieldcraft which were now to be put to the test under fire. He made his way out of the rear platoon positions and scrambled and ducked over the hard ground until we lost sight of him.

It was lucky he went when he did, for shortly afterwards a loud commotion arose in that locality and we found that the Japs had by now infiltrated at least one platoon into the few straggling bamboo huts in a hamlet behind us and marked on the map as Ywathit. Their intention was to surround us completely and to destroy us if we attempted to retire.

They got the shock of their lives.

The naik in charge of the section nearest to these intruders was one of the best NCOs in the whole company, by name Jitbahadur Gurung. He was big for a Gurkha and had always been a model of smartness and efficiency.

This NCO waited for no orders.

Shouting to his section to follow, he led a bayonet charge straight down the sloping ground at the Japs. So determined was the rush that the momentum carried them right through the huts. But the enemy did not wait to contest the issue. They fled ignominiously. Unfortunately Jitbahadur was wounded in his right hand, losing his trigger finger, and had to be evacuated after the battle. Thus we lost a magnificent soldier who was later awarded the Indian Distinguished Service Medal for his gallantry.

Little Krishnabahadur Ale, who was evacuated at the same time because of his dreadful head wound was recommended for the Military Medal, but for some unknown reason, it was never awarded. Jemadar Jitbahadur Ale gained the Military Cross for his unselfish gallantry in covering the section at the beginning of the fight. I also received the award of this medal.

For the next four hours our battle went on, during which time several attacks were thrown back. After one such attack, I raised my head to take stock of affairs and found myself staring at the body of a Jap who had fallen only a few feet from our position. A grenade had landed at his feet, between his legs, and blown him into eternity. The force of the explosion had not only maimed him but also the proximity of the burst had burnt his flesh and scorched his tattered clothing.

During all those hours, as we lay on the arid ground, the sun was beating down without mercy and the heat had to be experienced to be believed. I was told later that in the area 120 degrees Fahrenheit was quite usual. The only water we possessed was in our personal water bottles with a small reserve in the pachals carried by the platoon mules. I began to worry about the water supply should the fight continue indefinitely. So great was the heat that, at one time, I put my hand in my haversack for a bar of chocolate that I had preserved there. It had melted completely and soaked right through the webbing fabric.

Another NCO distinguished himself greatly during these proceedings. Havildar Bhombahadur Gurung was the platoon havildar in the forward platoon with me and, all during the action, he scrambled about in the open, hauling up extra boxes of grenades and ammunition, filling spare machine gun and tommy gun magazines, and eternally exhorting all and sundry to stand firm like true Gurkhas and fight. At the very beginning, when the section had been forced to retire from the ridge to our front, tears of shame had glistened in this NCO's eyes, as he feared a general retirement, but now he was proud and happy. None could fail to respond to his magnificent example. He, too, was recommended for a decoration but never received it. I am sorry to say that he gave his life under similar circumstances towards the end of the campaign.

Explosions in the village itself now denoted that our little rifleman had got through safely to the Colonel and that he was directing our artillery support into the village, as I had requested. One more Japanese attack came in upon us but they failed to penetrate our position. All this time we were still ourselves under sporadic shellfire and I was surprised to see that several of the shells that fell on us were duds. They landed with a nasty crump, but instead of exploding with a bang, they rolled over and over until they came to rest. We gave them a very wide berth indeed.

It was now mid-afternoon and we were digging for all our worth. I was anxious about what was going to happen when it got dark because darkness would rob us of our field of fire. The Japs would then be likely to infiltrate up the wide bed of the chaung, splitting my rear and forward platoons. What I needed most now was another platoon or two to fill in this very dangerous gap.

As if in answer to a prayer, I suddenly caught sight of a winding column of troops entering our rear platoon position during a lull in the shelling. At their head, as guide, came Captain Pat Davis from HQ. Strung out in his rear was the whole of 'A' Company with their commander Major Mike Tidswell and Scott Gilmore.

It was a heartening sight.

In addition to Gurkhas, there were machine gunners from the Frontier Force Rifles, who had been due to join us when the battle started; also, a British Artillery officer with his small group of British NCOs and soldiers as observers for our artillery supporting fire. They all came pouring into our position to join our band of exhausted but exhilarated men. I was now able to fill in those gaps which worried me and I now had a platoon in reserve should the Japs penetrate the perimeter. The heavy machine guns were sighted without delay and the artillery officer lost no time in taking compass bearings on the Jap guns, after searching for their flashes.

All these preparations going on simultaneously raised our morale considerably. The place began to look like a fortress and, sure enough, when the Colonel saw the positions later, the code name 'Fort' was coined and used in all subsequent references and orders.

There was a little sideshow during all this activity. Right up in front of our new arrivals were two men carrying a large stretcher and they hurried forward straight up to where I was standing. Seeing me quite unharmed, they looked surprised and confused, and pointed to my bush jacket which was covered in the blood of Krishnabahadur Ale. It transpired that the young rifleman who had got through with the message had described vividly how badly wounded I must be to present such a sight. I believe that he had convinced the Colonel that I was at my last gasp – hence the influx of officers. Certainly, they all seemed rather startled to see me walking towards them.

The pangs of hunger now manifested themselves and, not least of the highlights of that extraordinary day, was a grand meal which I shared with the British troops. For some time I had been eating Gurkha food which consisted in the main of curried goat and rice. Now, I sat down to eat British rations of fried bacon, fried bread and beans, followed by the inevitable mug of hot tea. When I lit a cigarette afterwards I felt like a king. It so happened that I was

never terribly keen on the curry and I could never polish off the
large helpings of rice which my orderly used to dish up in my mess-
tin or on a banana leaf. As he would take the remains away, he
would always shake his head and cluck his tongue to scold me.

By the time darkness fell our foxholes had taken shape and
digging was completed. As usual, as soon as the short, tropical
twilight descended on us, we stood-to and manned every post in
utter silence. I made my way round the platoons to check that
everyone was alert and prepared.

After checking the forward platoons, I crossed the sand to inspect
the rear positions. Just by one of the machine gun sites there was a
very small pagoda on a small mound and I stood there talking to
the jemadar from the Frontier Force Rifles who had made the
locality his own little HQ within our position. The whole landscape
about us seemed peaceful and quiet and it was difficult, in these
closing moments of daylight, to believe that a fierce battle had that
day raged over the ground, only a few hours previously.

In the midst of our chat we heard quite plainly in the still evening
air a whistle from over to the right of the forward platoon, answered
by a similar whistle from the left flank. We looked at each other,
but before either of us had time to frame a query a Jap machine gun
started firing. There was no mistaking the target as the bullets
zipped past all about us. We wasted no time in heroics but took a
headlong dive into a nearby slit trench, right on top of a burly
Gurkha officer whose face was a study as we both landed on top of
him.

For minutes that machine gun never seemed to stop. Burst after
burst passed overhead and we were literally unable to raise our
heads over the lip of the trench. We could hear the mounting racket
as other guns joined in. Realising that an attack seemed imminent,
it was imperative that we should get back to our posts and we had
to wait for a respite before we did so.

Before complete darkness surrounded us, the Japs made their
first rush on the forward platoons, but became entangled in the
barbed wire which we had strung out in front. Unlike the massive
wire entanglements of the Great War or those similar defences with
which I had trained in the London Rifle Brigade territorials before
the war, our use of wire was suited to the occasion. It consisted of

individual strands, concealed at ankle height in grass or bush and sown in a criss-cross pattern to a depth of several yards around the positions. The attacker, in daylight, with his eyes fixed on our foxholes, would fail to see it until tripped headlong to fall at our mercy; the night raider would not see it at all. The creeper or crawler, at night, seeking knowledge of our defences, would often become hopelessly entangled and betray his presence by rattling the tincans which we often would attach to the wire and fill with stones for greater effect. We also created booby-traps by slipping hand grenades into the large round cigarette tins of that era, after removing the retaining rings. When bumped, the tin would roll and release the grenade, often with spectacular effect.

On this occasion the Japs persisted in their attack after dark and soon scores of them were floundering about in the wire. To add to their misery, one of the platoon havildars, on his own initiative, began to fire Very lights up into the sky. These illuminated the whole scene in a weird and eerie magnesium brilliance and revealed the frantically struggling figures close to us and the fainter background of advancing, determined Japs, unaware still of the wire.

It has never been assessed how many of them died, because, as the night wore on, they made tremendous efforts to remove their dead, a practice at which they were adept. It was customary for a dead Japanese soldier to be cremated and his ashes, where possible, returned to Japan. In consequence, in all their engagements, they went to extreme lengths to recover bodies, often at the cost of more casualties. One must grudgingly admit that they showed great bravery on these occasions and also in their efforts to succour their wounded. One feels compelled to compare the cold-blooded fanaticism of Japanese commanders who condemn their men to certain death in suicide jobs with the equally practical efforts made to recover their corpses. It was a sure indication later of the collapse of the Japanese armies when more and more dead were left behind, and wounded prisoners also began to fall into our hands.

I was now back at my own command post and in charge of the defences. I found it necessary to call the Colonel on the field telephone which had been established and ask for more artillery fire to be brought down on the defensive targets. This is a system where likely enemy forming-up areas are noted and marked on the artillery fire plan as possible targets.

The response to my request was immediate and gratifying. The horizon behind us was lit up by the flashes of the 25-pounders and the shells sailed overhead in volleys to crash on to the Japanese attack, which was once more repulsed. After several abortive attempts to overrun us the Japs finally abandoned the big attack although small jitter parties operated all around us for the rest of the night.

There was no sleep for anyone that night.

CHAPTER NINE

Rat Hunt

When morning came it dawned upon us that the battle was won. As we looked out over the scene before us, the landscape had assumed once again the tranquil appearance which belied the feverish and violent activity of the night. No Japs were in sight, and it was impossible to say whether the village of Milaungbya was full of Japs or empty of all life.

Soon after dawn and still another anxious stand-to, a pencilled message* was brought to me from the Colonel. He sent his congratulations to the company for throwing back all the attacks and conveyed also the congratulations of the brigade and divisional commanders. The message went on to stress particularly that we must secure as many identifications as possible from Jap bodies or prisoners as the General considered that fresh Jap troops must be facing us to have put in such fierce and sustained attacks upon us.

I made arrangements for a strong fighting patrol to go out to comb the area around our perimeter for such identifications. In the middle of briefing the patrol, however, word reached me that the Colonel himself had arrived at our position and I arose to meet him.

He was unquestionably glad to see us all safe and sound. Colonel Walker, however, was never one to lose sight of his ultimate task, and he re-iterated his demand for identifications. He confirmed with enthusiasm the idea of the fighting patrol and suggested that his personal bodyguard, Havildar Kesharsing, should assume command of it.

This havildar was very well known in the battalion as the Jester in the nautches or dances which took place during the Festival of Dushera. He would leap about and gambol during the festivities and keep the audience in fits of laughter by his mimicry, much of which used to portray individual British officers and their personal foibles. In military matters, however, Kesharsing was no fool. He

* See Appendix II.

Sikhs fighting through Kyaukye.

Pegu in March 1945. The Japanese occupied the caves dug in to the hillside.

(Left) Gurkha returning from a fighting patrol which made contact with the Japanese on the Sittang Bend.

(Below) Gurkha Mortar team in action on the Sittang Bend, July 19__

was a physical training instructor in his own right and like so many of that fraternity he was as hard as steel and tough to boot. The Colonel had hand-picked him as his personal bodyguard and also appointed him to be in charge of the Guerrilla Platoon which was trained for special assignments.

Under the critical eye of his havildar, therefore, the patrol made its preparations and slipped out of the perimeter on what the Colonel nicknamed 'The Rat Hunt'.

Gradually they cleared the ground in front of the rear platoon and then edged their way over the ground lying between us and the 'C' Company positions to our right. The sandy bed of the chaung here was very wide and covered by quite tall, reed-like grass and odd stunted bushes. It was nasty, treacherous ground in the sense that it would afford good cover to the enemy and was in fact the ground over which the Japanese had attacked the day before. It was with some suspense, therefore, that we watched them spread out and advance through the grass.

A rifle shot suddenly rang out, and the leading Gurkha rifleman fell flat on his face, shot through the chest.

The Jap who had fired at point-blank range leaped to his feet out of the grass and bolted back towards Milaungbya. As he ran he was joined by another, and the two of them twisted and weaved through the grass in an astonishing fashion. Kesharsing at once dashed forward and killed one of them with a burst from his tommy gun; the other disappeared from his sight and was lost to view. He reappeared further on, visible to us, but obscured from the patrol by the grass.

At once, by common consent, we all opened fire at him and the next few minutes were quite extraordinary. The Jap twisted and turned, doubled back and forth and ran in circles as if demented, pursued everywhere he turned by spurts of sand as our bullets thudded about his feet. He literally hurled himself from scraps of cover to cover, rolled over and over, and stumbled on in an epilepsy of fear. At the height of all this excitement I found that not only were the rifleman firing at him, but the Colonel and myself had both grabbed rifles in addition to the Gurkha officers, one of whom manned a Bren gun. In spite of all the fire directed at him and two small mortar bombs pumped out by the platoon 2″ mortar, that Jap escaped. In a last despairing heave he threw himself down and rolled into a sunken track leading to the village; thus he passed out of our sight. How he lived, I shall never understand.

As the Jap vanished, our lust to kill seemed to evaporate as quickly as it had arisen. We all looked sheepishly at one another as we reckoned mentally the score of rounds of ammunition which had been fired at him. It was indeed a strange episode and put me in mind of a tale which I had heard previously from a regular officer in the regiment. He had told me that the Gurkha love of *'Shikar'* or hunting was famous and that in peace-time it had been known for a complete company on the march to break ranks and chase a hare that had scuttled across their path. On its escape or capture, either of which is immaterial, the whole lot of them had resumed march discipline as if nothing had happened. After witnessing and indeed participating in this Jap affair I have no cause to doubt his word.

No more live Japs were killed by the patrol but several bodies yielded the identifications which we sought. Our riflemen returned with Jap rifles, helmets, cartridges, cartridge pouches, bayonets, pay books and carrying with them a wounded Jap prisoner.

I knew that up to then no live Jap had yet been taken by the battalion and I was pleased at this turn of events. The men were in no mind to treat him gently after witnessing the death of our rifleman, and they carried him in like a sack of potatoes. There were four Gurkhas, each holding one limb, and they dumped him roughly on the ground in front of us. I noticed at once that one of his legs was badly smashed by bullets and he had obviously been lying out all night after receiving his wounds.

At first I was not sure whether he was alive, as his eyes were closed, but I called for a water bottle and dashed some water in his face. His eyes fluttered open for a second or so and then closed again. I opened his uniform tunic and put my ear to his chest to find out if his heart had stopped beating, at which he opened his eyes again.

Again I put the water bottle to his lips, indicating that he should drink, but he would not open his mouth and turned his head away. I turned it back and was met with a look of such venom from his baleful eyes that I realised that all kindness was wasted. I am positive that the Jap willed himself to die. Not a word was spoken but he just glared at us with hatred to the bitter end. After some ten minutes, in spite of our efforts at resuscitation, his eyes glazed and he fell back dead.

The manner of this man's death gave me to believe the then current stories that a Jap taken prisoner is regarded by his comrades and his family as dead. The Japanese either die in battle or return home victorious. To be taken prisoner is a slur on their courage which cannot be effaced, so they consider it more honourable to die.

This particular Jap's clothing and effects provided us with some valuable information. To our surprise, one of the first things to be removed from his pockets was an Army notebook full of the most revealing sketches of our own positions. There could be little doubt but that he was an NCO in the Intelligence Section of his unit and that he had been lying up for some time sketching our defences. The sketches were clear and remarkably well executed. These were sent back together with his pay book. His helmet yielded, after careful search, a beautiful silk Japanese flag of generous size, rolled up and pushed into the crown. In addition to the large red Japanese sun in the centre, the white surround was covered in Japanese hieroglyphics which I have since discovered were good luck messages from friends and relatives; this flag now hangs in my study, a tangible reminder of those far off and extraordinary days.

I was interested not only in these spoils, but also in this particular Japanese himself. So many of them looked positively bestial to our eyes, and somehow sub-human, with their close-set, slanting eyes and their large jaws full of buck teeth. But this man's features were akin in many ways to those of a Gurkha. He had a fair olive skin, rather than yellow, and above all he was clean. The unmistakeably Japanese distinguishing mark was his jet black hair which had been cropped short but was beginning to grow again in a straggly urchin like manner that I became to associate always with Japs. I found myself wondering what he was in civil life, as he somehow gave me the impression of being a civilian in uniform – perhaps an artist? Wherever he came from and whatever he was, his allotted span of life was now over. We buried him in the bed of the chaung and over his grave we stuck a stick holding a piece of cardboard bearing the legend *'Ek Japani'* ('One Japanese').

In the course of their search our patrol had reached the small rise in front of us from which the Japanese machine gun had caused us all so much trouble and which had wounded little Krishnabahadur. In their hurry to retreat, the Japs had taken the gun with them but had left behind two boxes of ammunition. I examined these with great interest. Unlike our Bren gun, which takes a vertical magazine, this Jap gun took horizontal clips of ammunition, the individual bullets being held rigid by raised projections stamped out of the metal, one to each bullet. Each clip was in a cardboard holder, rather like a box of crayons, the removable lid being secured by plastic tape, thus sealing the holder hermetically and rendering the contents immune to damp – a vital consideration in the monsoon in Burma. Each clip that I examined showed bullets as bright and polished as when they had left the factory. Dozens of holders were packed in strong wooden boxes lettered in Japanese and having stout rope handles. The efficiency of this race had to be admired.

Later, we captured the very gun itself and found it to be a beautiful piece of mechanism. It was a heavy machine gun, mounted on wide tripod legs, but what was fascinating to us was its fine balance. You could traverse the weapon from side to side through 180 degrees merely by the touch of a little finger. It was in perfect condition when it fell into our hands and we actually trained a crew to man it and afterwards it was used with telling effect against the Japs themselves. Later still, another similar gun was captured during one of our attacks and the two became permanent fixtures in the battalion. The Colonel would allocate them to any company going into the attack or to forward defensive positions of critical importance.

At the time, these two guns put me in mind of two trophies of war standing outside the regimental mess in Quetta. They were two 7-pounder guns dating from the Tibet Campaign, generally known as the Younghusband Expedition, of 1903/4 and they had long been christened 'Bubble' and 'Squeak'. I cannot honestly remember whether the Jap machine guns were ever christened or whether we were just glad to have them.

Our task was now defined in two parts – to shield the Irrawaddy bridgehead from counter attack, and to destroy the Japanese army where we found them. The first part of this task was being accomplished every time we threw back a Japanese attack during the next few days and nights, but to destroy the Japs in large numbers required that we should pass from the defensive frame of mind to the offensive.

For this purpose the Colonel obtained further permission from high authority to plan a series of 'killings' which he organised in great detail and put into effect with extraordinary success. Already being ahead of the brigade, it was not desirable that we should advance any further, and our line was accordingly stabilized for the present as semi-permanent. In this fashion the build-up of 'Fort' went on until we were certain that it would take a very large and determined Japanese attack to overrun us. We patrolled vigorously ahead and away out to our flank to villages named Legan and Pyingyaung and thus, quietly and unobtrusively, we gained mastery over the surrounding area.

The lessons of our intense patrolling practice away back at Kohima were now invaluable. The patrols moved out in small groups of two or three men and criss-crossed the land about us. The tit-bits of information which they brought back were pieced together with care and infinite patience until we had a clear picture of where the Japs were and in what strength.

During this time, however, the enemy did not leave us alone. Whilst he refrained from any big daylight attack, his artillery continued to shell us frequently and the artillery OP in our position was kept constantly busy trying to determine where the Jap big guns were sited. At a later date, whilst leading a night patrol, I was to stumble on one of those gun pits and the well-dug trenches only to find that the gun and crew had moved to another position. We became accustomed to this shell fire which gradually fell into a regular pattern of early morning, midday and early evening hate. One was almost tempted to picture the Japs as indulging in an afternoon siesta but this was not so. They work like ants and their bravery is equalled only by their industry.

Our own artillery tried constantly to knock out the Jap guns and sometimes the air above us was whistling with shells travelling in both directions at once. On these occasions a corner of my mind would idly speculate on what would happen if two shells met head-on. A long chance, but an interesting one.

At night the Japs probed our defences with their jitter parties. The jitter party is intended to scare the wits out of the defenders and also to make them reveal their dispositions by frantic and ill-judged firing. The psychological effect is strong.

As you peer into the darkness with straining ears and breathing under careful control, one may give scant thought to a hoot like an owl until it has sounded from several different positions. The brain debates whether it is a bird flitting from place to place or is it the signal for Japanese platoons to tell each other that they are now in place for an attack?

Nothing happens for a while; then, just as you may have dismissed the thought from your mind, an ear-splitting yell will pierce the night with anguish, summing up visions of some unfortunate sentry transfixed by a bayonet or garrotted at his post.

As your hair begins to creep on your scalp, you may be treated to a fusillade of shots from the opposite flank, followed by sundry shouts, commands or entreaties, often in English or Urdu: 'Charge', 'Surrender', 'Show White flag' are phrases which have all figured in these attacks.

The only successful answer to a jitter attack was ruthless self-discipline. Not one, single, solitary shot must expose your position. Such discipline under these conditions is the ultimate test of jungle fighters of any creed. It must be ingrained into each individual in training; to learn it in action is a costly business indeed.

We were not merely passive defenders. On this and subsequent occasions a few hand grenades silently and swiftly hurled in the direction of the loudest performers often worked wonders. Furthermore, each man, NCO and officer in the battalion carried some two dozen 'Panjis' for defence purposes.

The Panji is a bamboo stake some twelve inches long, by one inch wide, and sharpened to a needle point at one end. At the tip it is hardened like steel by the application of heat.

These would be 'sown' carefully in the ground around our positions with only a few inches of each one protruding above soil level. The effect of this deterrent on Japanese feet, clothed in their soft rubber patrol boots and crawling around our positions may easily be imagined, especially if hastened on their way by a grenade.

The shrieks and howls that used to echo around our foxholes at night were sometimes quite involuntary.

CHAPTER TEN

Milaungbya

After three days we received orders for the first 'killing'.

The village of Milaungbya was still the heart of the Japanese opposition from whence they would issue out to torment us; so this was our first objective.

First of all, I was told by Colonel Walker that the attack would be launched from my company position at 'Fort'. Consequently, I had constructed for him a command post in our forward platoon overlooking the ground in front which sloped gently down towards that village. It was revealed that we would receive support from the tanks of the Gordon Highlanders and the next preparation was a conference of all officers, platoon and section commanders, at which a model of the ground and the village was produced and used to illustrate the plan of attack in detail.

Tanks were a scarce commodity in Burma and in consequence each one was deemed to be priceless. It was customary for them to laager in safety back at divisional headquarters or thereabouts until actually required. This made sense. It would have been crass stupidity to expose them to infiltrating jitter parties for no particular purpose.

In order to ensure surprise, therefore, it was necessary to cover the noise of their approach from behind us until they were actually on top of the Japs. For this purpose it was arranged that a squadron of our aircraft should fly over us before the attack was launched. The aircraft would bomb and machine gun the village whilst the tanks lumbered up to our positions. This ploy was put into effect with success.

Next morning the battle commenced at 0800 hours.

From my company position, 'C' Company moved out to the attack in open formation after a small rise to our front had been cleared of Japs by a platoon under Subadar Kharakbahadur

Gurung, the same officer who had previously brought in the Japanese head. This Gurkha officer led his men with typical dash and ferocity and they took the rise with grenades and bayonets. From our command post we could see them clearly with the naked eye, rushing the foxholes, tossing in grenades, dropping to the ground whilst they exploded, and then dashing in to finish off the Japs, some of whom were stunned, wounded or paralyzed by fear.

War is not a pretty sight. It is horrible, animal and revolting. The lust to kill is savagely primitive and engenders a temporary madness in all concerned. Men shout, cry, whimper or blaspheme; they froth at the mouth and shine with the sweat of their unholy exertions; some carry on quite unaware that an arm has been shot away, others drop to their knees staring stupidly at an ever spreading pool of blood staining the ground beneath them; sometimes they die without a word, sometimes they start to scream as comprehension dawns on them and their life trickles away with their blood.

As 'C' Company advanced on the village from the left flank, three tanks accompanied them with guns firing to engage the Japs.

In no time at all the Jap artillery opened fire at these targets and both men and tanks were enveloped in clouds of smoke as they closed in on the village.

My job was to follow up this attack with my company as soon as fighting started within the village, and I now left the command post and deployed my company, ready for the follow-up. The Colonel who was frantically busy keeping in touch with the tanks and with 'C' Company on the separate wireless sets spared a moment to wish us luck, and off we went.

My little Gurkha signaller walked ahead of me with the wireless set strapped to his back; I had the earphones adjusted over my ears so that I could talk to the CO as we went. The Japs were ready for us and as soon as we appeared out in the open down came their shells upon us. The unfortunate signaller was a young lad going into his first set attack; as the first shell came screaming over, his reflex action was to fling himself to the ground. Quite a natural inclination, but unfortunately his wireless set was joined to my ears by the earphones and lead and I was pulled off balance and stumbled to my knees on top of the youngster.

The Gurkha officer, moving near me, thought that I had been hit by shrapnel and rushed across to do what he could for me; when he saw what had happened he lashed the lad with his tongue, yanking him to his feet with some obscene Gurkhali swearwords and helping me also to rise. The boy was covered in confusion, I was not quite sure whether my ears were still in place, but finally we recovered our poise and plodded on to the accompaniment of the screaming shells.

By this time the village was on fire and I could see men of 'C' Company vanishing into the smoke; bursts of small arms fire denoted that they had come to grips with the surviving Japs. We could clearly distinguish tommy gun fire, which always indicated close-quarter fighting.

We were not moving over the ground quickly enough for the Colonel whose voice kept booming in my earphones for more speed. We were not progressing fast enough for him because my company, strung out over a large area, had to execute a right turn through 90 degrees under shell fire in order to come in and hit the village at the right spot as planned. To do this on training is one thing, but in the confusion and racket of battle both platoons and sections are liable to lose touch. I had to resort to blowing my whistle at intervals to effect the desired result. I soon learned that my whistle and lanyard were not mere ornaments for mess dress.

As we came right up to the village, we found the destruction much greater than when viewed from afar. As a result of the aircraft bombing the whole place was crackling with flames and a dense pall of smoke arose for hundreds of feet into the air. The ground beneath us was ankle deep in ashes and burning cinders which scorched our boots and the legs of our battledress; half the bamboo bashas had collapsed under the impact of the bombs and our paths were blocked by crackling and exploding timbers of bamboo which created a blazing inferno and impeded our advance.

The village was divided into two parts by a sunken track which ran through from east to west and the plan was for my company to reach this track and protect the rear of 'C' Company whilst they continued their attack.

Once inside the village, however, all was confusion. In addition to the burning bamboo, the noise was deafening; the huts, compounds, hedges paths and trees all reduced visibility to a few yards; at once my flank platoon was out of view. Signals were useless so I had to keep in touch with that platoon by runner. Having once more established contact, I now gave the order to advance to the sunken track, where I hoped to catch up with Peter Myers and his men.

Sure enough, as we advanced through the chaos and reached the place, I caught sight of him and his second-in-command, crouched on the track and watching their front. There was a big dip in the ground and at the other side a larger pagoda stood some fifty yards off on a rise. A Jap machine gun dug in a bunker there was causing casualties and holding up the general advance. I crept forward and tapped Peter on the shoulder to indicate that we had arrived.

Although a Bren gunner was at this moment engaging the bunker, the Jap gun continued firing at any head that was raised over the bank of the track. Peter Myers had therefore informed the tanks over the radio link and was waiting for one to deal with the pagoda.

At this stage I halted my company and settled down to watch developments. Sure enough, one of our tanks came smashing its way through trees, hedges and bamboo huts to engage the bunker from the flank. The Bren gunner endeavoured to identify the target for the tank by firing tracer bullets which somehow added still another dimension to the unreality of the scene around us.

While this was going on, I became aware of shouting to our right along the track. I glanced over and was stunned by what I saw. Jemadar Jitbahadur Ale, in command of that platoon, had either received no message to halt or else had misunderstood our plan. He seemed to be convinced that we were to pass straight through 'C' Company to continue the attack, which was often the case in training.

The shouting which came to our ears was from his whole platoon charging down the slope towards the pagoda, with this gallant officer out ahead in the lead. They were heading straight into the cross fire of the tank and also of the Jap gun. I was horrified. I jumped up onto the bank, waving my arms and blowing my whistle for all I was worth.

Somehow the sound reached Jitbahadur, who looked back, and

whose mouth dropped open to see me standing up there giving the field signal for about turn and retire. He may have thought me crazy, but an order was an order to a Gurkha. He came to a skidding halt and waved his men back. They also must have thought him mad but their discipline triumphed and they came back to the track.

The tank accomplished its mission and destroyed the Jap bunker position, crushing the whole construction of logs, sandbags and sods of earth right into the ground. 'C' Company were then able to resume their attack to clear the Japs clean out of the village. In the usual circumstances we would have occupied the village and consolidated the position, but in view of our orders we returned to our lines after mopping up the remaining Japs who fought to the bitter end.

Instead of returning to 'Fort', my company now changed places with 'C' Company so that we were in an entirely new and different type of position. Our trenches were some 500 yards from the village of Milaungbya so that we were in extremely close contact with the Japs. Whereas we had previously been out in the open country, we were now amongst trees and vegetation bordering the chaung estuary.

It was an uneasy position since the area was fringed with bushes and undergrowth which gave the assailants a covered approach right up to our foxholes on one particular side. It was not feasible, however, to destroy this undergrowth since it did at least camouflage our own positions so we had to depend on our sentries to be very alert and to give us warning in time.

Those Japs must have been puzzled by our actions. After we had withdrawn from the village they lost no time in infiltrating back again in small parties, and by nightfall they were in some strength. In the still evening air we could hear distinctly the sounds of their digging and a steady hammering as they repaired their shattered bunkers.

Patrols from my company edged forward in twos and threes and actually observed them at it and pinpointed their strong points.

We ourselves were not idle.

We felled several lofty palm trees which we used to strengthen and roof over our own bunkers in which the Bren guns were sited.

This activity continued until late into the evening. We also acquired from Battalion HQ a section of the Pioneer Platoon who had been specially trained in laying booby traps. They worked away like ants, putting down their tricks in the undergrowth and amongst the barbed wire; after dark we settled down to await events.

That night was extremely dark and you could hardly see your hand in front of your face. About midnight, the silence was shattered by a violent explosion just in front of one of our bunkers. Remembering not to fire their rifles, our men tossed over several hand grenades in that direction and were rewarded by two loud screams, and then dead silence. To investigate was out of the question because of the dark and our own booby traps, so we hopefully awaited for further developments. Nothing at all happened and we were unmolested for the remainder of that night.

Next morning, at dawn, we could hardly wait to see what might be revealed. As the darkness lifted and the shadows dispersed, we saw several objects on the ground only some five yards away from the bunker slit. On approaching closer, we saw a Japanese helmet, a rifle, a long bamboo pole, some square blocks of guncotton, and some orange coloured cloth such as worn by Burmese monks and which had been used to bind the blocks together. There was blood on the cloth and marks on the ground as if some object had been dragged away over it.

It was clear that the Japs had sent a patrol to stalk our bunker with an explosive pole charge. If thrust through the slit and detonated it would have wrecked it and killed the men inside. Fortunately, the enemy ran into the booby traps and the grenades and must have been severely wounded. Perhaps one was killed and the other had abandoned his rifle in dragging him away. The men in the bunker were surrounded by their comrades and looked rather sick as the others laughed with typical Gurkha humour at their discomfort.

The following night the Japs probed our positions again, but took the precaution of driving a few cows in front of them. Needless to say, these animals set off several of the booby traps with the result that we were standing to most of the night in expectation of an attack.

Next morning I was involved in rather an embarrassing incident.

My Subadar called me over to where one of these poor animals was standing in the wire, badly wounded and with one leg shattered. He indicated that the animal was beyond aid and I agreed at once. Then, without thinking, I said: 'Go ahead, Subadar Sahib, shoot her.'

He looked at me quizzically, fidgeted and looked down at the ground. Suddenly it dawned on me just how stupid I was. The Hindu regards the cow as a sacred beast and here I was making this off-hand blasphemous suggestion without due thought. Clearly, there was no one else to despatch the animal in my company, so I had to do it myself.

Without relish for my task, I unslung my tommy gun. I determined to make a nice clean quick job of it with one shot. Raising the gun, I aimed carefully just behind the beast's shoulder and gently squeezed the trigger. Unfortunately, in my embarrassment, I omitted to check that the gun was set at single shot. The gun shuddered in my hands and a stream of bullets hit the cow which collapsed at once, riddled from shoulder to tail.

For the next few weeks activity was constant around the battered remains of Milaungbya. It has been officially stated:

... Meanwhile, 89th Brigade, which was disposed to prevent a Japanese advance on the bridgehead from the Chauk direction, was beating back determined Japanese counter attacks. At Milaungbya, four miles north of Singu, the 8th Gurkhas killed 250 Japs, a record bag being 94 in one day ...

During this continuous battle the battalion gained the following awards:

3 Military Crosses
2 Indian Distinguished Service Medals
2 Military Medals
2 Certificates of Gallantry.

The organised 'killings' continued, sometimes with the aid of tank support; sometimes without support. On one occasion my company had taken part in a daylight infiltration attack into half of the village, supported by our 3″ mortars, firing over our heads from behind us like a small edition of artillery. Frank Crouchman was in charge of these mortars and was firing them for the first time in this fashion.

We met with a certain amount of success and killed a few Japs but were halted by fairly strong opposition in the vicinity of the sunken track that divided the village. We were approaching it from the opposite direction to the previous occasion.

Whilst the mortars were firing, I found myself lying near a crater made by a 500 pound aircraft bomb during one of the previous attacks. The Japs in vacating this particular spot seemed to have thrown into the large hole a lot of interesting-looking boxes, some articles of equipment and the odd steel helmet. There was also several yards of the saffron-coloured cloth filched from some Buddhist monastery. It was a souvenir hunter's paradise.

Several of the men nearby had noticed these articles and one or two had crawled over to investigate. Some inner sense gave me warning and I felt uneasy at this offering of loot. I crawled closer still and gazed on all the junk. My suspicion was confirmed when I detected the glint of a piece of wire leading from under a steel helmet and disappearing down into the jumbled articles. It was a massive booby trap waiting to be sprung by some inquisitive rifleman. I waved the men back and tossed in a grenade from a safe distance. The resulting bang set off a series of explosions from Jap grenades cunningly hidden under the pile.

This incident took my mind back to an occasion in the training centre in Quetta when we were shown a film on booby traps and I was thankful for the caution it had sown in my own mind. I had always remembered that particular film and the last fade-out shot. A patrol has found a house (European) and gone through every known precaution about entering and searching the rooms quite safely. Finally, confident that the place is safe, one man enters the WC. Instinctively, he pulls the chain... up goes the house.

On another occasion, 'A' Company, under Mike Tidswell, who was later killed, mounted a frontal attack on the village from my own company area. On this occasion I was a mere spectator, staying in the command post from which the Colonel was directing the battle. It was quite a big affair with tank support on the flank to cut off any Japs who might run, and with an Auster spotter aircraft overhead to direct our artillery on any Jap movements in their rear. In this little plane was an Artillery Observation officer whom we had all come to know personally from previous battles.

The previous night I had been asleep in my bunker when my orderly shook me roughly by the shoulders. As I opened my eyes he hissed in my ears: 'Japani tanks ayo!'

Japanese tanks? I bounded out of the bunker and dashed forward to the most advanced post where a Gurkha rifleman was pointing forward into the darkness. I listened intently. Sure enough, I heard a regular, steady clank, clank of caterpillar tracks over the night air. It was an ominous and frightening sound. The noise seemed to be coming from out in front, but a little over to the left, between 'Fort', now occupied by Peter Myers' company, and our own positions. If this was Jap tank support coming up they must be about to launch a big attack. Our own attack was timed for 0900 hours next day. Who would strike first?

I immediately checked that our one anti-tank weapon, the PIAT, was in position and then went back to my bunker. I picked up the field telephone and spoke in low tones to Peter Myers. He confirmed that we were not dreaming and added: 'They seem to be moving towards you, old boy. Best of luck.'

I then got through to the Colonel who was woken out of his sleep to hear my tale. At once be brought down our artillery fire on the village, and in a cross pattern about it, and the night was rendered hideous by the screeching and bursting shells. I could visualise those gunners woken out of their sleep, and leaping to their guns, already ranged, and I thanked my lucky stars for the efficiency and co-operation of modern war.

When the last echoes of the bursting shells had faded, I listened carefully, with head cocked on one side. Darn me if I didn't hear that infernal clank again.

We gave them the treatment once more and they took the hint. Silence fell on the whole countryside, but none of us slept again that night.

Next morning, just before 0900 hours our aircraft struck the village whilst our tanks were rolling up from the rear; we got our attack in before the Japs. This was the day that 94 Japs were killed,

A Naik gives a Burmese woman a cigarette after the liberation of her village.

A pause in the fighting — members of the 4/8th Gurkhas display Japanese trophies.

Rifleman (later Havildar) Lachhiman Gurung VC, 4/8th Gurkha Rifles.

one of the reasons being that they had been bringing their reinforcements up to strike us and they were as thick as fleas upon the ground. It was estimated later, when the scene of carnage was inspected, that they had as many as five or six men in every foxhole. Our attack had pre-empted the enemy strike by the narrowest of margins.

The aircraft supporting us were Hurricanes and each carried a single 500 pound bomb which was released on their first run over the village; on every other run they used cannon fire which was really awe-inspiring to hear. There was an angry crackling roar about cannon fire that spelled destruction and the Japs in that small target area received the full brunt of it.

As soon as the last plane had fired its last shell, it turned and came roaring down in a dummy run to keep the Jap heads down. This was the signal for our attack and the Gurkhas surged forward, shouting their warcry: '*Ayo Gurkhali!*'

Despite the destruction wrought by the planes, there were plenty of Japs to meet them and the fighting was fierce. In the rush men on both sides were dropping, and a concealed Jap machine gun on the flank held up the advance by its very accurate fire.

This did not please the CO. Impatient at the delay, now speaking on one wireless set, now on another, he turned suddenly to our young Signals Officer who was also in the command post and rapped out: 'Mr Logan. Go forward and for God's sake find out what's holding them up!'

This was an unexpected and tough assignment for the youngster who had not been in action before. Sensing this, the second-in-command, Major Watson-Smyth, volunteered to accompany this young officer and they set off together. In seconds they were out in the open and had covered perhaps twenty yards when a burst of Japanese machine gun fire sent bullets crackling over from the flank and whipping past their heads. Lieutenant Logan's Gurkha felt hat gave a jerk and only his chin strap saved it from floating away; a bullet had drilled a hole clean through the crown.

Both of them dropped to the ground and were pinned there for a while, although just at this moment the advancing company chose to push on. We signalled to them to return as we engaged the gun and they scrambled back to the safety of our position. Needless to say, young Logan was speechless, and could only point to the bullet hole in his hat and stutter. I knew exactly how he felt.

While this was going on, the tanks out on the right flank in the open ground towards the Irrawaddy came on the air and reported signs of Japs breaking out towards them. As those tanks had been placed there for just such an eventuality they met them with point blank fire from all their weapons.

Simultaneously, the little Auster aircraft which was circling overhead also came on the radio. We could hear distinctly the voice of our Artillery friend through the large wireless set.

'They're running! They're running!' he yelled, and as he went on shouting his voice rose higher and higher in pitch with his excitement, like a Derby commentator. He shouted map references and descriptions for our benefit and our artillery fired at once on his instructions.

'That's it!' yelled the voice, 'Right amongst the bastards. That's beautiful!'

Perhaps the excitement overcame him, or perhaps the plane hit an air pocket. I don't know. Next minute, however, the unfortunate man was violently sick all over the cockpit and we heard the whole performance on our wireless. We could hardly believe our ears.

In the meantime we were not getting away scot free in the command post. The Japs, in their desperation, started firing at us with an artillery piece at point blank range. The shells were bursting right inside my company perimeter and unpleasantly close to us. They were firing over open sights from under 500 yards, with a whizz-bang effect.

This was something new and nasty. That gun had not been there yesterday, I thought, and suddenly I remembered the noises in the night. It was not Japanese tanks approaching, but tractors dragging up the artillery under cover of darkness, ready for their big attack. So it proved.

That gun gave us a hard time but as suddenly as it had started firing, it stopped and we found out afterwards that it had been spiked by the crew just before they fled. It fell into our hands that day and wires were also discovered leading from the gun position to a concealed observation post overlooking our positions. No wonder the shells were dropping close.

During all these hectic days I had paid several visits to the Battalion HQ at different times and for different reasons.

To start with, the water question was acute in our front line positions. We had no supply whatsoever on the spot, and every day the battalion water truck would visit each company to fill up the waterbottles, packals and chaguls. A packal is a square metal container and there were two to each platoon, loaded on either side of the platoon water mule. The chagul is peculiar to the Indian Army. Originally, it was no doubt an animal skin for holding water, but the Army issue was made of canvas and shaped not unlike a water bottle (domestic). You soaked it and then filled it with water which kept amazingly fresh inside for quite a while.

With these limited supplies, therefore, a bath was quite out of the question. When I visited the battalion HQ I always made straight for my great friend Tony Brand Crombie, the Quartermaster. He and I had known each other in Quetta and we always had plenty to reminisce about on these occasions. His Gurkha orderly, Ratnabahadur, invariably put the kettle on whenever he saw me coming down the track; and then he would prepare a bath for me. This was primitive, but provided real luxury for me in my filthy condition. Ratnabahadur had dug out a hole in the ground in which a canvas sheet was placed. Into this he would pour the bath water and overhead he had a contraption which, with the aid of a biscuit tin, provided a shower. Emerging totally refreshed, I would then have a mug of neat rum, if available, stuck into my hand by Tony. It was not quite like our 'tonks' in the sophisticated atmosphere of Quetta, but it was mighty good at the time.

One day I arrived there just as Tony was arranging to go back to Divisional HQ at Pagan. He asked me if I would like to go along for the trip. I jumped at the idea; a change of scenery would do my battle-weary mind a lot of good, I thought.

We set off in a jeep for this ancient city and soon left the battalion far behind us. My feelings were like those of a schoolboy released for the holidays. On arriving at Pagan, we made straight for the Ordnance Depot where Tony had made arrangements about stores and weapons.

It was near the Dump that an incident occurred which, though trivial, was at the same time aggravating, although I have smiled about it many a time since. After interviewing the appropriate people, we were emerging from the Dump when we caught sight of a mobile tea van manned by two ladies of the WAS(B) [Women's Auxiliary Service (Burma)]. There was the usual small queue waiting to be served consisting of Divisional HQ clerks, storemen and similar personnel.

We thought that a cup of tea would be welcome and we strolled over to join the queue.

One of the good ladies looked sharply at us. Seeing that we were strangers, she acidly informed us:

'We only serve front line troops here. Do you belong to this HQ?'

For a moment I was nonplussed and at a loss for a reply. But not so Tony Brand Crombie, who exploded:

'It may interest you to know, Madam, that my friend here was in action against the Japs less than eight hours ago. He has come back here for a change of scenery.'

The WASBIES did a splendid job in Burma, but some of them on occasions showed rather a lack of imagination. I am reminded of the story of the bearded Sikh who was offered a razor blade in lieu of small change, and his endeavours to convince the good lady that it was of no use whatsoever to him.

CHAPTER ELEVEN

Fantasia

The 1st April 1945 was a red letter day for us. On that day, after nearly six weeks continuous fighting, the battalion was at last brought out of the front line and occupied the village of Nyaungla, some four miles to the rear. This was in the vicinity of Brigade HQ.

The spot was very pleasant, the village being situated on the banks of the Irrawaddy and the mess being housed in a good Poynggi Kyaung, once occupied by Burmese monks. Nearby we found the battery from 136 Field Regiment under Major Clark. These were the British gunners who had given us such excellent support during all our troubles in the front line; a finer bunch of people you could not find. They admired the Gurkha, the Gurkha liked them, and their officers and ours might well have belonged to the same unit, so intimate and friendly was the give and take.

For two weeks we enjoyed ourselves, resting the men and refitting. It was now three months since we had set out from Kohima during which time we had constantly been on the move, culminating in the last six weeks of intense fighting. Boots had worn out, uniforms had rotted away with constant daily soaking with sweat or had been torn by jungle thorns or cactus hedges. Peter Myers and Tommy Logan might even have had a chance to exchange their bullet-holed Gurkha hats for new, but I do not remember them doing so. Even I, who had discovered a nick on the brim of my own hat, would not have parted with such a souvenir.

One of the pleasures of this period was to take trips on the river in local boats fitted with outboard motors and manned by the battalion motor transport personnel under the enthusiastic command of Captain Willie Willox, our very popular MT officer from Scotland. So successful were these trips that we began to be referred to as the Nyaungla Flotilla. Bathing, the mobile cinema and local concert parties provided the rest of our amusements.

One of these concerts staged for our benefit was given by some Burmese dancers and proved extremely popular with the Gurkhas. Two outstanding incidents remain in my memory. One was a sword dance performed by a slim Burmese girl who parried and thrust like lightning against an imaginary foe. The way she twirled her sword seemed to impart to it a living entity of its own as it flashed and circled her shoulders. At one time I could have sworn that she had three swords in her hands; but I freely admit that I was totally mesmerized.

The other item was a Burmese choir who sang some fascinating songs of their own and then, as a finale, broke into a refrain that somehow seemed vaguely familiar. Amidst the clashing of cymbals and the wail of flute and pipes accompanied by the thudding of hand drums, I tried to identify the tune, but it escaped me. The language did not sound like Burmese. I tried to concentrate. Suddenly I made out the two words 'Bonnie.....ocean.' They were playing 'My Bonnie lies over the ocean', which was followed by 'God save the King' – all in our honour.

The Gurkhas applauded every single item and those who appealed especially to them (particularly the little dancers) received rounds of thunderous applause, together with a shower of coins and cigarettes for which they were duly grateful.

In the middle of this happy evening a shocking tragedy occurred.

In Burma we carried our weapons at all times, even whilst taking recreation and on this occasion we were sitting with them between our legs. After one particularly good act, one of my jemadars jumped up and down with excitement as he applauded. He must have banged the butt of his gun on the wooden floor beneath him because the safety catch disengaged, his sten gun exploded and a burst of bullets entered his stomach. He was carried off for an emergency operation and I finished that hilarious evening walking up and down outside a tent whilst the doctors battled for his life. I felt stricken when they finally emerged shaking their heads. My platoon commander was dead.

During this period the battalion was given one task in the shape of maintaining a patrol base of one platoon on the west bank of the Irrawaddy in order to patrol forward parallel to the river. It is necessary to explain here that on that side of the river, some twelve

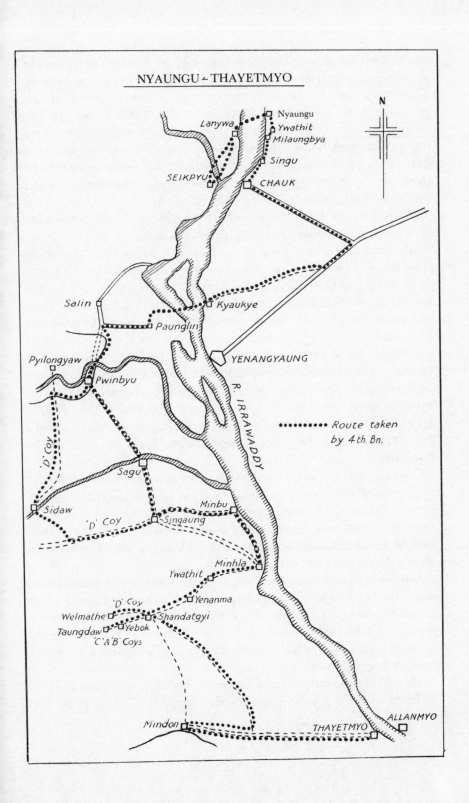

NYAUNGU – THAYETMYO

N

Lanywa
Nyaungu
Ywathit
Milaungbya
Singu
SEIKPYU
CHAUK

Salin
Kyaukye
Paunglin
YENANGYAUNG
Pyilongyaw
Pwinbyu

R. IRRAWADDY

·········· Route taken
by 4th. Bn.

'D' COY

Sagu
Sidaw
'D' Coy
Minbu
Singaung
Minhla
Ywathit
Yenanma
'D' Coy
Welmathe
Shandatgyi
Taungdaw
Yebok
'C'.&'B' Coys
Mindon
THAYETMYO
ALLANMYO

miles downstream was the village of Seikpyu, situated at the end of an all-weather road leading from the Japanese forces in the Arakan. This road was of two-fold importance. First it provided the Japanese with an escape route from the Arakan, but in the meantime some fifteen miles up that road were the nearest Allied troops who were being savagely attacked in what was known as the Letse Box. So, by using this road the Japs could either reinforce the troops at Letse or they could bring them back to cross the river to Chauk and reinforce the troops fighting us. At this stage the 1/11th Sikh Regiment had taken over our old positions and were endeavouring to advance on Singu and Chauk.

My company was chosen to establish the patrol base across the river and Captain Pat Davis, the Intelligence Officer from HQ, was ordered by the Colonel to accompany it. It was an important task because any information gathered by the patrol would be of great consequence not only to the battalion but also to Brigade and Division.

I chose No 4 Platoon, commanded by Jemadar Manbahadur Gurung. The platoon was the unfortunate one which suffered from our own shelling during our first battle, but Manbahadur was a man of great courage, a typical squat Gurkha with a direct approach to any problem. After his experiences with this platoon, Pat Davis later rated the platoon as perhaps the best in the battalion.

The site for the patrol base had been chosen by the Colonel who had crossed the river with Pat Davis on reconnaissance the day before. When Pat crossed again with the platoon the engine of his ageing assault boat broke down and for about ten minutes they drifted down towards the Jap territory. However, it did restart and finally disgorged them on the far bank.

Pat later described that side of the river as a moonscape, consisting of a maze of broken hills, rising some five hundred feet above the river. It contained a series of sharp ridges which were devoid of soil, vegetation or human occupation. From a military point of view it was something of a nightmare. The heat was almost unbearable.

Patrolling was duly carried out for several days and then Pat was relieved by Scott Gilmore with a platoon from 'C' Company. On

Easter Sunday, 1st April, Pat relieved Scott and on Easter Monday he made a really memorable patrol, penetrating the twelve miles to the outskirts of Seikpyu and back and securing valuable information. After reporting back to Brigade and to General Evans who was visiting them at the time, Pat was again sent across the river on 7th April, this time with one of my other platoons. No 7 Platoon was commanded by Jemadar Jitbahadur who had already been recommended for the Military Cross after our first battle. He was what was known in the regiment as a 'Line Boy', i.e. he had been born, not in Nepal, but in the regimental lines. He was extremely intelligent, very cheerful and had an excellent command of English which was practically unknown in a Gurkha in those days.

At this time, the Brigadier was pressing our Colonel to produce a Jap prisoner for interrogation purposes. Pat Davis had already told Walter Walker that during one of his probes into the Jap-occupied country, he had passed a large red house near Lanywa, between the patrol base and Seikpyu; in fact, the patrol had once been fired on from the vicinity of the house. This was enough for the CO. He instructed Pat to take a 'snatch party' and abduct a live Jap from the Red House positions.

Setting off with a havildar and three men in the late evening, Pat reached the vicinity of the house by dark. Biding his time, he waited until night had set in properly. Leaving the three men behind and accompanied only by the havildar, he stealthily climbed the hill on which the house stood. Together they moved slowly all round the building. There seemed to be nothing. No wire, no trenches, no Japanese.

There was a tarmac road leading from the house down in the direction of Lanywa and Pat and the havildar moved silently along it in their rubber patrol boots. After covering about 100 yards, they heard voices. These came from a bunker partly dug into the ridge above the road. Whilst the havildar covered him, Pat crept still closer until he found himself actually on the roof of the bunker itself. Surprised that there did not seem to be any sentry on watch outside the bunker, Pat was nearly overcome by the temptation to drop a grenade down a ventilation shaft but caution prevailed. The object was to snatch a prisoner and he decided to return with more men the next night, as originally planned.

The two of them carefully withdrew and rejoined the remainder of the patrol. As they started back down the slope one of the men below Pat slipped and started a small avalanche of stones bounding downwards. Suddenly, only a few yards away from Pat, a voice called sharply. He was so startled that he took an involuntary step backwards, lost his footing and found himself falling. He rolled over and over in the dark as a rifle shot cracked out above him, followed by another. The element of surprise had certainly been lost and to tarry any longer would have been a useless exercise. At the bottom of the steep rocky slope Pat gathered the patrol together and set off for home.

Next night Pat set off again with another havildar and the men of No 5 Platoon. His plan was to send two sections to the right of the bunker whilst he with another section would make a demonstration from the opposite side, hoping to drive some Japs into the waiting arms of the patrol. They covered the familiar miles to the valley below Red House without incident and started to climb the hill. Halfway up the slope they split as arranged. Just as they reached the vicinity of the bunker, moving in complete silence, there came the sounds of a Gurkha trying to catch up in a frantic hurry; scurrying footfalls, the rattling of small stones, heavy breathing. Pat turned round in anger to hiss at the man behind him, so that he in turn could hiss at the man behind him and so on. It was too late. There was a hoarse challenge from a few feet above, a rifle cracked and the bullet flew just past Pat's head. Cursing his luck, Pat now had to act fast. He drew a grenade and lobbed it into the slit of the bunker where it exploded. Yells and screams came from the bunker, followed by the thud of running feet. Then silence. If the plan was working, those Japs would be running into the other two sections cordoning their retreat. For minutes Pat listened intently for some kind of noise which would indicate this. Instead, a fusillade of shots rang out, many of which came whistling over their heads. Then more silence.

Success in a venture like this has to be immediate. Hit and get out is the maxim. In the dark, with the Jap bunker between the sections, there was no real way of knowing whether the snatch party had actually grabbed a Jap. To tarry now invited Jap grenades to be rolled down the hillside accompanied, perhaps, by machine gun fire. They were all very vulnerable on the bare, rocky hillside. Pat made his decision and fired a red Very light into the sky. This was the signal to get out to the rendezvous.

On arrival at the RV Pat's fears were confirmed. The Japs who had fled had not followed the track towards the Red House which the havildar and his men had blocked. They had escaped at right angles over the ridge. This more direct route to their other posts might have been covered by Pat and his section had the alarm not gone off prematurely. There was only one casualty amongst the Gurkhas – a naik who had twisted his ankle coming down the hill.

Two days later a local Burman stated that the patrol had killed two Japs and wounded three. The Japanese in Lanywa were furious and had accused this Burman and others of betraying them.

The other incident concerned 'A' Company when their turn came to man the patrol base. Our American friend, Scott Gilmore, set off from the base on a very arduous trip indeed. His objective was to make Seikpyu and back, covering in all twenty-four miles of rough going during the night.

The night was pitch-black, the terrain horrible; but they made it there and back. I happened to be standing next to the Colonel when they had returned and were reporting to him over the large wireless set next morning. I could distinctly hear Scott's travel-weary voice speaking in hollow tones.

'Patrol Base calling. Patrol Base calling. No 9 please. Over.'

'No 9 speaking. Over.'

'Say, Colonel, we made it. It's twelve miles there and twelve miles back; but we made it. Over.'

'Yes. Yes. Are the Japs there? Over.'

'Sure they're there, Colonel. We lay down and observed them. Several lorry loads of them came down the road with their lights on. I estimate fifty to a hundred. Over.'

'Good. Did you hit them? Over.'

'Say again. Over.'

'Did you hit them, Gilmore?'

'Er... Well... No... Colonel. To tell you the truth we were so shagged out by our little trip we could raise no enthusiasm. Over.'

Beside me the Colonel's face turned purple, but he stifled his emotions. Such frankness is refreshing, after all. We now knew what we wanted to know. It was a reconnaissance patrol, not a fighting patrol. If they had got involved twelve miles away from their base and near to dawn, they would have had a very sticky time. Scottie was just applying American logic to the situation and American frankness to the telling of it. No double talk in his make-up.

The Colonel pressed the switch again.

'All right, Scott. Get some sleep and come back over the river to-night. Your relief is ready. Over.'

'Wilco. Out.'

Subsequently, Scott's remark about 'we could just raise no enthusiasm' became a catch phrase amongst us for quite a long time. At a later date, Scott demonstrated more than a fair share of enthusiasm when he took over command of 'A' Company in the middle of a battle when Mike Tidswell was killed by a Jap sniper. His guts and determination under fire so impressed Colonel Walker that he actually promoted Scott to Major on the spot over the wireless.

As we now knew for certain that the Japs were being reinforced ahead of us at Chauk from across the river at Seikpyu the information was sent to the members of the Special Force who had arrived in the area. Little is ever heard of the splendid work done by such men and it is my privilege to put on record at least one of their successful operations.

These men manned canoes in the bows of which were mounted machine guns. They would then let themselves drift down the Irrawaddy on the strong current to watch what the Japs were up to. They chose a dark night and found hectic Jap traffic across the river.

Choosing their moment well, they opened up on the unsuspecting enemy and succeeded in sinking a large raft on which was lashed a Japanese field gun, in addition to killing some and wounding more of its crew.

They all returned safely.

At last our rest in the pleasant surroundings of Nyaungla came to an end and we were ordered forward once more in order to relieve the 1/11th Sikhs.

Since taking over from us a fortnight earlier, they had been trying to capture the next village, Singu, and had managed to press on to within two miles of it. However, the Japs had excellent observation and subjected the Sikhs to accurate shell fire daily, combined with harassing attacks by their infantry. The forward Sikh positions were astride an isolated hillock which bore the appropriate name Fantasia; no wonder. Whoever invented this codename had hit the nail on the head. In front of the position was an undulating stretch of country leading to the village; barren, open and arid. Overlooking the position from beyond Singu was a large escarpment which rose high into the air in a line of cliffs across a wide chaung and from which the Japs could see virtually every movement around Fantasia. After experience of jungles and mountains, to be isolated in that unhealthy spot gave one a true feeling of fantasy, unreal and as if suspended in time.

The battalion now received orders to capture Singu.

We gathered for our last conference in our comfortable Ponggyi Kyaung, preparatory to advancing forward, and the Colonel picked my company for the job.

It was decided that to attempt an attack in daylight under the eyes of the Jap observers on the cliffs ahead would be a costly business. I can imagine that in the First World War battalion after battalion would have been flung into the holocaust which such an action would invite, but in our war as a rule commanders were not willing to sacrifice their men to no purpose. It was decided therefore that we should infiltrate by night into a strong position in the centre of the village, making the approach from the eastern flank.

On the morning of 14th April we moved forward, through our old positions and the battlegrounds of Milaungbya, the scene of so much sweat, blood and sorrow.

The mere routine take-over from the Sikhs was in itself a delicate business. We crept down the edge of the one road, a few feet at a time and a few men at a time, relieving section by section. Our supplies had to be carried by hand, after dark, as either motor transport or mules would have presented simple targets. As it was several Jap shells came screaming over and landed on and near the road as we moved in; whether it was the daily dozen or whether they had spotted our own stealthy movements I will never know. Whilst all this was going on, the battalion moved up to their old positions in the Ywathit area, not so very far behind us.

My orders were to move out of Fantasia and advance against the Japanese at midnight, but the spearhead of our infiltration was to be a platoon under command of Pat Davis who had recently been posted to my company. Having another British officer with me had now relieved some of the mental strain which I had been feeling earlier when isolated with only my Gurkhas around me. Thinking in, and speaking in, Gurkhali for long periods at a time inevitably imposed such a strain.

I wished Pat good luck as he set off with Jemadar Manbahadur Gurung and his men of No 4 Platoon. He left in daylight as he was going to do some patrolling and deception before our main effort at night.

By about 1500 hours they had succeeded in establishing themselves on a small hillock surrounded by trees some three hundred yards from the village. From here Pat sent out a couple of three man patrols into the outskirts on the west side. His intention was twofold: to find out whether there were any Japs on this side of the village and their strength; also to distract them from the eastern approach which we were going to use. The patrols reported Japs in small numbers and one of the patrols was fired on.

Darkness came at last. Pat gave the orders to move and the platoon vacated the hillock and moved silently up the chaung between Fantasia and Singu. They had only moved some half a mile when a tremendous racket split the night air. Rifles, machine guns and grenades were banging away to the accompaniment of Japanese yells. A full scale attack was going in on the position which they had just left.

Pat Davis had two signallers with him, reeling out telephone cable, to keep in touch with me at my Company HQ. My plan was to feed him No 6 Platoon, under Jemadar Jitbahadur Ale, as soon as he had gained a footing in the village. It was slow work as the patrol could not move faster than the two men carrying the heavy cable drum. At last, however, my field telephone buzzed and Pat's voice, low and hushed, informed me in a whisper that he had established his platoon where required. Jitbahadur immediately moved out with his men.

The overall plan required me to wait for 'A' Company to send two platoons to take over Fantasia before I could follow up. I waited and waited, with time slipping by. Over an hour passed and my anxiety grew. Every hour lost meant an hour nearer daylight and the risk of being caught in the open. At last I contacted the CO on the wireless and was told that they had left ages ago. There was only one thing to do. I sent a scout back on foot to try and trace them. He returned within a few minutes to confirm that he had found them halted in the dark only some five hundred yards behind us. They were waiting for orders. By the time the misunderstanding was resolved we had lost valuable time which was going to cost us dearly.

At last they filed into our positions; again, a slow and laborious business conducted with great stealth lest the Japs should get wind of movement in the still night air. I now set off with my column which consisted of quite a large body of men. I had No 5 Platoon, my own Company Headquarters, an Artillery Observation officer and his party of gunners, together with another party of heavy machine gunners from the Frontier Force Rifles. There must have been between fifty and sixty men moving in the darkness. A small patrol such as I normally would lead can move quietly and quickly but I was concerned about this mass of people with all their paraphernalia.

Our advance consisted of an encircling march far out to the left flank of the village so as to come at it from the east, effecting surprise. My intention was to strike it at the point where Pat Davis was waiting.

As we moved over the open ground my fears were confirmed. The gunners were reeling out telephone cable for communication and the metallic sound of the cable drum unrolling produced a horrible, regular, monotonous clank clank which to my horrified ears seemed to be audible for miles. I gestured violently to them to muffle it but the beast seemed to have a will of its own. It seemed to grow louder. In addition, men here and there started to stumble in the darkness;

their boots rang on stones, water bottles thumped on hips and bayonets scabbards slapped against thighs. My scalp began to crawl with more anxiety.

We had some distance to cover and, as we were already late in starting, time was against us. We pushed along as fast as we could, but I still had to make the detour fairly wide. This combination of factors was unfortunate.

At last, shortly before dawn, I spotted the outline of the outskirts of the village in front of us. A small cluster of pagodas lay nearby. I did not want the dawn to come up behind us and silhouette us for Jap eyes in the open, so I made for the pagodas, each of which was surrounded by a low wall about three feet high. Halting in their shadows, as the dawn broke across the sky, I studied my map and sent a two man patrol forward to find Pat Davis. It transpired later that he was some 800 yards away along the edge of the village.

As the grey light strengthened, there came the crackling outburst of rifle fire from the line of trees and plantations lining the edge of the village. Machine guns joined in and I could see Japanese figures running forward at us.

The attack was so sudden that we were caught off balance for a moment or two. But fortunately, as of one accord, we all leapt over the small encircling walls of the pagodas and put the brickwork between us and the Japs. One of the machine gun teams of the Frontier Force Rifles, with commendable alacrity, flung themselves down in the open, mounted their gun, and commenced firing back; but a burst of Jap fire killed the crew. The bullets hit the No 1 on the gun in his head and his steel helmet shot several feet up into the air; he must have been wearing his chinstrap behind his head during the march.

Our own weapons were now all firing over the wall. As I peered out at the Japs I found that in those first few moments I had automatically seized a hand grenade from my pouch and pulled out the pin ready to throw it. It was still clasped close in my hand and I had dropped the pin in my leap over the wall. The Japs had now withdrawn to the shelter of the trees and were firing to keep our heads down for their next rush.

Still clutching the grenade, I was in a dilemma.

If I could not find the pin I would have to throw the grenade and

A resupply – an essential element in the fighting in Burma.

(Left) 1945. Major Peter Myers MC, and Major Peter Wickham, 4/8th Gurkha Rifles. *(Right)* Subadar (later Subadar-Major) Krishnabahadur Rana MBE, 'C' Coy. 4/8th Gurkha Rifles. 1945.

Gurkhas probing a Japanese foxhole.

waste it or risk dropping it by accident and blowing myself up. A ridiculous personal problem in the midst of the far greater one facing us all. By one of those hundred-to-one chances I caught sight of a glint on the ground beneath me and there was the pin with the ring attached. Even now it was tricky putting the pin back in, but I managed it without mishap.

Meantime, the Japs had placed snipers up amongst the trees and they were peppering us with bullets all about us from their vantage points. The wall was losing its value as a protection from view. As we sprayed the trees with our Bren guns, a sharp-eyed young rifleman standing next to me spotted one of the Jap snipers. He grabbed my arm in his excitement and pointed frantically at the exact tree. Just at that moment he fell back with a gurgling cry and blood frothing at his lips. I laid him on the ground under the wall; as I did so, another Gurkha who was firing the Bren gun on the other side of me collapsed silently over his weapon with a small hole drilled in his forehead. Another of our Bren gunners switched his fire at once to the tree and the bullets seemed to strip the branches as they lashed through them. We were rewarded by seeing a Jap body somersault from the top and crash to the ground.

I was now trying to render first aid to the young rifleman. Blood continued to froth at his mouth and his every breath drew forth a ghastly sound from his punctured lung. I stripped off his tunic and saw a small blue hole at the top of his chest, just below the shoulder blades. This was also frothing slightly with blood. I wondered where all the copious bleeding was coming from that was pooling on the ground beneath him; when I put my arm under him to turn him over, I found a hole in his back large enough to put my fist in. This was where the bullet had torn out after piercing the lung and deflecting from a rib.

Shortly afterwards he died; but the Bren gunner took at least four hours to die; his agony was accompanied by pitiful moans and screams which we could do little to alleviate except by administering morphia. The bullet had lodged in the brain and he was delirious most of the time.

The position was now stale-mate.

Every time one of our heads rose above the wall, a bullet crashed into the brickwork or whistled past to thud into the pagoda; and yet we just had to keep the Japs engaged. In this manner we suffered more casualties. My only contact with the Colonel was over the wireless and I informed him of the situation.

Colonel Walker considered that we should stay where we were as, after all, we had gained a foothold in the village; he proposed to manoeuvre another company on the other side of the village to catch the Japs between two fires. He knew that our ammunition consisted only of what we carried and that we had not eaten since the previous evening. So it was imperative to send us our rations and ammunition; also to effect a link up between us and Pat Davis before nightfall. Evacuation of casualties was also now of vital importance.

In order to get across the open, vulnerable ground around us, in full view of the Japs in the village, three Bren gun carriers were borrowed from the gunners and they set out under the command of Major Geoffrey Bull. In spite of some very tense and anxious moments when all three carriers broke down one after another in the most difficult places, they finally reached us safely and took away our casualties.

The sight of the carriers may have been too much for the Japs; maybe they thought that these were the heralders of tanks to follow. Anyway, they cleared out without offering any further opposition to us and by last light we had advanced up to Pat Davis and his platoon. Strangely enough, they had been left alone during our fighting. Although we had parted only the day before, so much had happened in between times, we felt rather like Stanley and Livingstone; we were certainly glad to see each other safe and sound.

This was infiltration with a vengeance. We now held half the village; the Japs held the other half. Separating us was a deep cleft in the ground almost like a chaung and lining the rise on the opposite side were the Japanese positions. The whole situation was very unpleasant indeed. During the hours of daylight they swept our foxholes with fire; the men in the forward positions were forced to remain in those holes in the ground without relief.

Water was now the great problem. Our only supply was from a well in the middle of the village but this could only be reached by crawling along the ground in hazard from the Japanese snipers during daylight or by waiting until darkness.

The most active and the most accurate of the Jap weapons was a machine gun firing from a brick house and although we directed our fire against this place it did not silence this weapon. The gun stuttered into life at irregular intervals and when the house eventually fell into our hands I paid a special visit to the room from which the gun had been firing. The Japs had cut a hole in the thick brick wall through which the gun was pointing, and the machine gunner had been sitting in comfort in a curved back wooden chair and firing when he thought fit. The floor was inches deep in spent cartridge cases.

I put my eye to the aperture and could clearly see our positions and the excellent view which he had of them.

Next day, 'A' Company moved up and took over from us, and it was necessary to wait until dark before the men could extricate themselves from our trenches. At the same time 'C' Company took possession of some high ground to the east of Singu, after some token resistance by the Japs.

On 19th April 'A' Company spent a very unpleasant day due to accurate enemy snipers, and they suffered some casualties.

During these days preparations were in hand for us to put in a really big attack and clear the village once and for all. On the 20th we moved forward for this purpose but found that we were not making contact with the Japs. They seem to have disappeared during the night. We now received the order to continue our advance. As we swept through the village to the open ground beyond, the reason became apparent.

High up on the escarpment of cliffs ahead of us we caught sight of tanks on the horizon; their crews were waving frantically. They belonged to 33 Indian Infantry Brigade who had advanced rapidly against Chauk from the south-east and forced the Japanese to retreat back across the Irrawaddy.

The prize of the Burma oilfields was now within our grasp.

CHAPTER TWELVE

Irrawaddy Recrossed

The capture of the Burma oilfields was a glittering prize which capped the operations lasting from our crossing of the Irrawaddy back in February. It was also a reward for those who had fought from the swamps of the Arakan, through the mountains and jungles of Kohima and Imphal to this arid plain of Central Burma. In fact, I doubt if many of those who perished in those foul swamps or gave their lives on the mountain slopes could ever have foreseen this day in the most optimistic flights of their imagination.

There was nothing glittering about the sight that met our eyes as we marched into the little oilfield town of Chauk.

We had rested for two days in Singu which was so smashed up by the bombing and shelling that all tracks and paths were obliterated. Collapsed houses and huts, scattered masonry and corrugated iron sheets in utter confusion covered the whole village; we were thankful indeed that we had not met opposition in our attack. We were even more thankful when we discovered that beyond the village, some several hundred yards further on, the Japanese had constructed the finest labyrinth of trenches and bunkers that we were ever to see during the campaign.

All bunkers were constructed of massive teak logs riveted together by iron bolts and cemented into place. Fields of fire for the machine guns were cut out of the actual soil so that our attack would have been in view every inch of the way. I looked out from the inside of every bunker slit in turn and it required no imagination to picture our troops stumbling through the shambles of the village to emerge out into open ground swept by devastating fire.

Even the Brigadier acknowledged that in his estimation the attack, as planned, would have resulted in 75 per cent casualties. Leaving Singu on the morning of 23rd April in motor transport, we passed through Chauk and, as I have said, there was to be found nothing glittering in the sight. This was our first close view of the oilfields which we had seen in the distance for so many weeks; there was nothing to enthuse over.

Bare rocky hills, reminiscent of the desert, surrounded the town; the oil derricks, red with rust, unkempt and uncared for, leaned this way and that, raising their frameworks to the sky at distorted angles. A strong smell of oil hung over the whole district and added to the discomfort and the heat.

The Japanese had been in possession of all this valuable equipment for over two years and had apparently taken no steps at all to rectify and repair the damage we had inflicted on it all when we had retreated in 1942 and blown up the installation.

As we passed through, we saw evidence of peacetime bungalows, compounds and even a swimming pool but now it was difficult to believe that Europeans had spoken of Chauk before the war as a comfortable and pleasant cantonment. The one thing that did impress us was the tarmac road beneath our wheels after months and months foot-slogging over dusty tracks and across country. We now visualised advancing (perhaps even in motor transport!) all the way to Rangoon on excellent roads and through civilized countryside. We were sorely mistaken. The General had other plans for us.

We learned to our chagrin that whilst the rest of the Fourteenth Army was to advance in spectacular fashion, converging on Rangoon from north, east and west, we were to recross the cursed Irrawaddy River for the second time and in the opposite direction in order to clear the Japs from the country beyond the west banks. The Japanese still had the hard core of their Arakan Army on that side of the water and they would no doubt be attempting to break out across the river. The place chosen for our bridgehead was Kyaukye. After crossing the river we were to concentrate at Paunglin, some eight miles from the crossing.

The advance was resumed and after passing through Chauk we turned to the main Yenangyaung–Gwegyo road and fairly hurtled south.

The first night was spent near Milestone 181, and the next night at Laligan about six miles east of Kyaukye. The bridgehead had already been secured by the 1/11th Sikhs without opposition and we crossed on the morning of 25th April 1945.

As our little assault boats bobbed across the water, the first thing we noticed on the far side was a tank stuck on a sandbank. We ourselves had to scramble out on to another sandbank and wade ashore through the soft sand. On gaining the bank the first thing which we had to do was sit down, take off our boots and pour the water out. Our socks were soaking wet – a fine start to the march that inevitably lay ahead.

It was a boiling hot day, we were back on foot after our recent joy ride, all were marching with full packs and the journey to the concentration area was undoubtedly the most unpleasant and exacting that the battalion had yet been called upon to endure.

It was only eight miles, but the chosen route lay across country consisting of deep sand, ploughed earth, six foot high spear-grass, deep chaungs and swamps full of filthy, stagnant water covered in mosquito larvae, reaching to thigh level; the whole area abounded in leeches.

The sweat coursed down our faces, carving furrows in the thickly caked dust and trickling down our bodies to merge with our evil-smelling, swamp-soaked battledress trousers which clung wet and black about our limbs. As we marched on and on interminably, I thought of that lovely tarmac road leading on to Rangoon, now far behind us. Not for the first time in this war I cursed my lot and the whim which had led me to volunteer in the first place for the Poor Bloody Infantry.

By late afternoon it was a very sorry procession which at length arrived at Paunglin, only to find that the supply arrangements had broken down. No road had been found for the motor transport so neither tanks, artillery nor our own supplies of food, bedding and ammunition had arrived. There was no prospect of anything until next day.

The last straw occurred when the second-in-command, Major Bob Watson-Smyth, and Geoffrey Bull, in order to cross the last few hundred yards of swamp separating them from the objective, commandeered a country craft to row them across. The boat was light, their combined weight excessive, and after travelling a hundred yards or so the boat quietly settled down into the swamp, leaving the officers waist deep in mud and water, much to the amusement of the Gurkhas lining the bank. Mr Churchill's words regarding toil, sweat and tears were never better understood.

Next day, after a very uncomfortable night, we sorted ourselves out and the rations caught up with us. With them came information about the Japs.

They were at this stage withdrawing through a village named Salin towards the south, and the 2nd King's Own Scottish Borderers had had several small skirmishes with them. Another brigade, 114 Indian Infantry Brigade, advancing slowly but surely from the north were now only a short distance from Salin, driving the enemy before them. We stayed only one day at Paunglin before moving west to play our part.

The night of 28/29th April saw us take our next step towards contact with the Japs. It is also a night that we shall all remember because of an unendingly tedious march which lasted until dawn, all along the banks of a canal. The orders were to reach a village by the name of Pwinbyu which was the other side of the Mon Chaung. The crossing was to take place early after first light. Although opposition was expected from the Japs, it did not materialize, and we entered the village by 0800 hours.

In all our long trek of 500 miles from the Indian Frontier, this was the most attractive village we had come across. Green grass, tall trees and small canals lining the roadside all combined to make it an oasis after the dreadfully arid country we had left behind across the Irrawaddy.

Our reflections on the beauty of the place, however, were marred by a gruesome discovery, the first of the acts of Japanese atrocity to come to our notice. An Indian was discovered at the bottom of a slit trench with his hands tied behind him; his body was gashed and pierced by countless bayonet thrusts. It was a revolting sight, but it did at least show the Gurkhas that the stories about Japanese cruelty were not mere inventions or propaganda.

The battalion now took up positions south of the village, but 'D' Company pressed on for some three miles and halted south of another village, Pyilongyaw, which was reported to be held by the enemy. This company was to be separated from us for several days and was destined to attract a good deal of Japanese attention before they rejoined their comrades.

At this time, three officers arrived in the battalion as reinforcements from the Jungle Warfare Training School back in India. These were the first officer reinforcements which we had received since leaving Kohima. Captain Quentin Kennedy was an old friend of mine from Quetta days and he was also a great personal friend of Mike Tidswell. Neither of them was destined to survive. Lieutenants Peter Dickenson and Douglas Farnbank were retained for the time being at Battalion Headquarters and Quentin was at once sent off to join 'D' Company. He was to receive an immediate introduction to action.

In order to confirm a report that the Japs were in possession of Pyilongyaw, a small patrol from the company was sent there on 30th April. They reported that they had seen a small party of Japs south of the village and brought back a Jap head to prove their point. A further report indicated that some 500 Japs were in the village and this proved to be extremely accurate.

The company was next ordered to advance down the Sedaw valley and this they did at night, halting some twelve miles from Sedaw itself.

A jeep patrol was sent to spy out the land, but after covering only two miles they themselves were ambushed by the Japs and nearly lost the jeeps. The vehicles just got out in time and the drivers brought back the news. At once, the company commander, Geoffrey Bull, brought the company up in support and attacked the Japs without further ado. The whole of the day was spent in ejecting them from the village. Meanwhile, everyone was pleased to hear that the missing men from the patrol turned up safely after all.

By early evening the place was in our hands and every man was digging feverishly for protection before nightfall. It was a very unpleasant spot indeed, surrounded by thick jungle, and it was here that we lost the first Gurkha officer to be killed in action.

Jemadar Nathu Gurung was a platoon commander who had been into his company headquarters to receive the usual evening orders. Unfortunately, the conference took longer than was expected and it was dark when he set off to find his own platoon position. Thinking he was on the right track, he walked quite unknowingly outside the perimeter and was at once attacked by Japanese who were lying in wait to attack the company. They bayonetted Nathu through the stomach. Simultaneously, the company was attacked on three sides.

The unfortunate officer staggered into Company HQ with blood pouring from his wounds and, as he blurted out his story, the company commander thought that the platoon position had been overrun. As only thirty yards separated platoons from HQ it was assumed that the Japs were now inside the perimeter. Confusion reigned for a short while but fortunately they were driven off. Jemadar Nathu survived the night and was evacuated next morning. It is sad to relate that he died seven days later.

It became clear that the Japs had attacked this company in order that their main body might leave Pyilongyaw and press on towards the east. They managed to do so during the night and by next morning the road to Sedaw was open; the company reached there in the afternoon.

This village is situated at the headwaters of the canal, and some lavish accommodation was found there. It had originally belonged to the Canal Officer but was now enjoyed by all the company. After twenty-four hours' rest, they moved on across country to a main road where they were lifted in vehicles to rejoin the remainder of us. This road had only been cleared the day before by the KOSBs and tanks of the 3rd Carbiniers – with the loss of several tanks.

We were now advancing fairly rapidly to the south with the object of cutting off the Japanese Army from the Arakan. They were clearly making frantic efforts to cross the Irrawaddy to head for the border of Siam.

Two days of consecutive marches brought us to Minbu, on the bank of the river where we rested one night; and then on to Minhla. These were large, handsome villages with lush gardens and plenty of evidence of life in peacetime Burma. There was also evidence of Jap occupation, including a large Japanese stone memorial over a grave; perhaps some general had died there during the campaign.

The name Minhla also reminds me of a visit to Rochester Cathedral after the war was over. My wife and I were wandering in this silent vault of whispering stone when the name Minhla caught my eye. The name was part of an inscription on the wall: a memorial raised to the memory of a young officer who was killed in 1886 or thereabouts whilst leading a charge against this Burmese village. It was not difficult to visualise the young subaltern falling, mortally wounded, as he reached the stockade. What a debt this country owes to the unknown heroes of yesterday.

It was also near Minhla that I was involved in an unsavoury incident.

A Burmese driving a bullock cart was brought in front of me by a sentry. The Burmese kept gesticulating and pointing to the back of the cart, over which hung a black cloud of flies, but I could not understand a word of what he was saying. Thinking that he was perhaps trying to sell us some vegetable produce or something, I decided to inspect it before turning him away.

I approached the cart and removed the palm branches which were laid across it. To my disgust there was revealed the dead body of a Japanese whose head had been almost severed from his neck by a blow from behind. It was attached to the corpse only by a shred of skin at the neck. By now the Burman was smiling ingratiatingly and holding out his hand for reward.

Overcoming my nausea, I replaced the covering and directed him to battalion. Let them sort out this nasty little problem.

At this stage it is useful to consider what the Japs were trying to do so that future events may be seen in their true perspective.

To reach the Irrawaddy River, the Japs from the Arakan were side-stepping us eastwards to try and outflank us and reach the river. We, on our part, received explicit orders that we were to destroy them and we were therefore moving south-west to block the various valleys leading to the Irrawaddy.

Time was a vital factor in this game of hide-and-seek, and some very stiff marching fell to our lot. Our brigade moved off from Minhla with the 1/11th Sikh Regiment one day ahead of us, and we ourselves covered fourteen miles through an area of Reserved Forest before halting for the night. As we were to relieve the Sikhs next morning, I went ahead in a jeep to make contact with them and to learn the route; my task was to lead one company of Gurkhas in a march that night.

The Sikhs were at a place called Yenanma, a further fourteen miles ahead and the jeep covered the ground quickly. I did not particularly relish retracing my steps and covering it again as guide that night.

When I arrived at the Sikh positions, I found that only an hour previously they had laid a very successful ambush and destroyed most of a platoon of Japs who had been marching along the road. The Jap bodies were lying all over the road in grotesque positions, some with their bodies riddled by bullets, some with their heads shattered. Even the blood all over the road had hardly dried. It seemed to me extraordinary that so many could have been caught together in one place. The Bren gunner who had caused most of the damage was a havildar who was proudly demonstrating to all and sundry how he had caught them in his sights and waited with patience until they all had come into point-blank range. It was like a copy book lesson from the training manual. It was certainly a massacre.

That same evening the jeep took me back to the battalion just in time to swallow a quick meal and then set off, on foot, to lead 'B' Company over the route to Yenanma.

The march was wearying in the extreme, as are all night marches. To the physical exertion was added a nagging, persistent, thought that the Japs themselves were travelling down a parallel valley, perhaps at this very moment. Several times we came to tracks crossing ours at right angles and it was clear that they had come from that valley. As guide, I was naturally at the head of the column and it was with circumspection that I approached each crossroads. By the time we reached the Sikhs, at dawn, we were all weary, and I for one felt something of a mental wreck. At one time during the night we saw clearly reflected in the sky the beams of vehicle headlamps over a hill; the only vehicles showing lights in Burma at that time were Japanese.

Later in the day the remainder of the battalion caught us up, and as we were all on air supply at this time arrangements were put in hand quickly for an air drop. As the aircraft came humming over and the parachutes floated down, the Japs became really inquisitive and gave us a very uncomfortable evening by raining mortar bombs on the dropping zone. A few mules were killed and slight casualties caused amongst us.

The next day was VE Day.

We spent it at Yenanma, whilst the Sikhs moved to the next valley to repeat their tactics. 'D' Company of our battalion was sent out on a twelve-mile march to the north to report that area clear of the enemy. We all thought that it was a very poor way to celebrate VE Day.

By about midday it was discovered that we were all drinking water from a stream at a spot below the graves of the Japs killed the day before by the Sikhs and hurriedly buried there to avoid polluting the air in the great heat. Our reaction may be imagined. It was the last straw.

On the night of 9th May, one of our companies again moved forward to contact the Sikhs and this time arrived there early in the morning right in the middle of a fierce battle. The Sikhs inflicted heavy casualties on the Japs and very definitely denied them passage through the Shandatgyi Valley.

Next day we all followed up and by that evening the whole brigade was in the area of that village, with the exception of the KOSBs and one battery of artillery.

Once again the Japs side-stepped to the west and the stage was now fast being set for one of the fiercest and most prolonged battles ever fought by our battalion, a battle which brought to us the unique honour of the only Victoria Cross awarded to our regiment during the Second World War.

At stand-to the following morning, our Colonel paid a visit to my company and drew me aside. His orders were explicit:

'When we stand down, Denis, I want you and your company to be ready to move in thirty minutes. During last night, one of our patrols was able to carry out a successful ambush on Japs over to the west. They are heading this way. If you go quickly enough you may be able to intercept their main body in the vicinity of Taungdaw.'

As I listened to Colonel Walker, I ran over in my mind just what his orders entailed. In the space of thirty minutes we had to eat, pack up, load the mules with food, ammunition and water and be ready to move off. I studied the map. I estimated that the tiny hamlet marked on the map as Taungdaw was about twelve miles away. We had covered fourteen miles the day before over tough

Burmese country and spent the remaining hours of daylight digging in. The thought of another twelve miles after a hurried breakfast was repugnant.

  'Time is the vital factor,' the Colonel continued. 'You must reach Taungdaw without delay. My hunch is that the Japs may reach it within three hours.'

The assignment was even tougher than at first sight. It was clearly to be a forced march to carry out this order in the time. I called my platoon commanders together and rapidly outlined what lay ahead. We bolted our food, loaded up and were ready to go in the allotted time.

None of us will ever forget that march, pitting ourselves against the clock; pushing on with chests heaving; halts cut to a minimum.

All about us was an area of Reserved Forest up in the hills and the route we followed lay along a narrow track which skirted the side of a ridge. Every twenty yards or so a tree lay felled across our path, blocking it to mules or jeeps, but our column of Gurkhas moved forward relentlessly like some huge caterpillar undulating over these obstacles.

Whether the trees had been felled by the Japanese to impede our advance, or whether Burmese woodcutters were responsible we shall never know. It certainly impaired the thythm of our marching, but did at least relieve the monotony. The Gurkhas made light of it as I might have expected. They will, of course, laugh at anything and laughter is very infectious. The object of our forced march, however, was not a matter for humour.

CHAPTER THIRTEEN

Taungdaw

The name of this obscure Burmese hamlet – Taungdaw – is now enshrined in the annals of the regimental history of the 8th Gurkha Rifles. Every year the 12th May is declared to be a regimental holiday celebrated with parades in honour of those who took part in the battle, remembered with nostalgia by this ever decreasing band, and enjoyed as a day of sport and recreation and nautches by those who came after.

No clairvoyant vision of all this could possibly come to me as I looked down on Taungdaw from our vantage point nearly 1,000 feet above it on that far-off day in 1945.

My binoculars revealed no sign of Japanese but only the figures of Buddhist monks, in their saffron-coloured robes, moving about in the vicinity of their beautiful Poynggi Kyaung. This Burmese monastery nestled against the bank of a stream which flowed through the valley, far below. A track led in to the monastery on the other side of the stream from the direction of the next valley to the west. This would be the direction from which we might expect the Japanese to appear.

I decided to descend into the valley, cross the stream and thus interpose my company between the track and stream junction and any body of Japs coming from the west. Advance scouts were despatched down the mountain to the village, which was reported clear of the enemy. We then moved down the track in battle formation. The leading platoon found the stream to be fordable, the water reaching knee level, and they moved across without incident.

A few minutes later, the first rifle shots rang out.

Ahead, I had a vision of brown monks running helter-skelter for dear life away from their beloved Poynggi Kyaung. They ran through the lovely gardens and disappeared into the distance. Simultaneously, I caught sight of Japanese soldiers breaking rank and spreading out into firing positions astride the track. We had met them head-on as they came down the one and only escape route from the next valley. We had beaten them to this important track and stream junction by only minutes. Our forced march had paid off. It occurred to me that if they had motor transport with them, they would have to destroy us to get through.

In no time, the rattle of rifle fire was joined by the crackle of the Jap machine guns as they brought a light machine gun into action and our Bren guns replied with rapid bursts. There was no time to choose platoon positions; they were pre-determined by circumstances. As we went to ground out came the entrenching tools. I was glad to think that at least we were astride the water supply, although our tactical position was not good.

To anyone conversant with Japanese tactics it was possible to visualise the likely pattern of events. They would seek to cross the stream, out of our sight around the nearest bend, and then encircle us from the rear. All-round defence was therefore vital. I gave orders to dig in without delay, but these were hardly necessary.

Whilst the foxholes were taking shape, I had established contact with Colonel Walker on the wireless. He was grimly pleased to hear that we had made contact as he had desired. He asked me whether I was able to cope with the situation with my one company and I explained our poor tactical position, overlooked by the forest clad ridges above us. I also explained that although our position was bad we were actually blocking the track to the Japs and any motor transport. Colonel Walker told me to stay put. His plan was to send another company to our aid and he expressed the hope that we could hold out for the next few hours whilst they pressed on towards us over those twelve miles which now lay behind us.

After the first fierce exchanges, firing had become desultory and there were long intervals of silence which in themselves became nerve-racking. There was nothing more unsettling than the pregnant silence which often followed a Japanese attack. From experience we knew that they were always active and up to something. The favourite move was to encircle in ones and twos, in groups and sections. When the countryside offers such excellent cover for movement, the imagination might well run riot. It was easy to see in every breeze-ruffled bush and stirring grass the image of that squat peaked cap or dome-shaped helmet surmounting the ugly features of the Japanese soldier.

In our present position I was disturbed that if they encircled us too soon, our friends, rushing to our aid, might run into an ambush. A standing patrol was therefore placed out in the direction from which we had come to give ample warning. No further attack materialized during the next few hours and it was with relief that we welcomed those stocky Gurkha figures who at last appeared amongst us at the end of their long march.

This was 'C' Company; my old company with whom I had trained for so long at Kohima, when I had first joined the battalion. Their commander, Peter Myers, approached and we wasted no time and few words.

'Where do you want us to go?' he said. 'Shall we amalgamate and form a double perimeter?'

I thought rapidly. Twice the number of men manning our posts, which were rapidly taking shape, was a happy thought; but we were still overlooked by the dominating ridge opposite.

'Look here,' I replied, 'if you can get up there you could give us excellent supporting fire; if we start to alter our positions here the odds are that they may attack and catch us in the middle of the change-over.'

There was no real necessity to convince Peter. His battle-experienced eye could take it all in and already he was ordering his subadar to collect his platoons for the move up the hillside. Off they went up the steep slope looking over us, and we kept in touch by wireless. We were sorry to see them all leaving us so soon after their welcome arrival, but my faint misgivings were utterly dispersed in due course when the radio receiver crackled and Peter's voice came over the air.

'What a climb,' he said, 'but what a view. I can see your positions clearly from here and all the ground to the east of you. It's lucky for you that I am not a Jap OP.'

Interrupting these pleasantries, my signaller called me to the other, larger wireless set in charge of two Sikh signallers. This was the more powerful long-distance set which kept us in touch with the Colonel, twelve miles away. It was, however, subject to bad interference and atmospherics from the mountain ridges around us

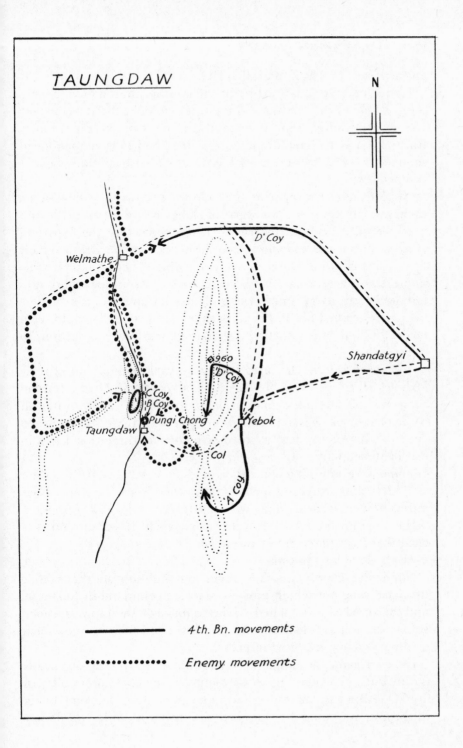

TAUNGDAW

N

Welmathe

'D' Coy

Shandatgyi

◇960
'D' Coy

C Coy
B Coy
Pungi Chong
Taungdaw
Yebok

Col

'A' Coy

――――――― 4th. Bn. movements

••••••••••• Enemy movements

and separating us from Battalion HQ.

I explained the situation briefly and informed him that we should now be able to carry out our initial task – to deny the Japs passage to the Irrawaddy and to force them to abandon their motor transport. Later events disclosed that they had indeed abandoned some forty trucks several miles back and had also carefully booby-trapped them.

Not long after my report to the Colonel, a shower of grenades fell upon our position without warning, followed by intense rifle and machine gun fire from the east. This denoted that the Japs had crossed the stream, as expected, and were now preparing to assault us. The shouting and screaming which accompanied this unpleasant phenomenon revealed that they were some eighty to a hundred yards away and working themselves up into a frenzy. Our men were trained not to fire back unless they actually could see a target and only a few scattered shots rang out from our sections in reply.

I glanced around the faces I knew so well, looking out of their foxholes, their Gurkha hats slanting across their heads, hinting somehow of discipline and pride of regiment. That quizzical, Mongolian look was on each face. Here and there an upturned eyebrow, here and there a broad grin convinced me that I was in excellent company.

Some were squinting along their rifles, easing the butts into their shoulders and searching for a target; others were loosening their kukris in their sheaths; some were placing grenades in a convenient niche cut into the forward lip of their trench. It was abundantly clear that a warm reception awaited our enemies.

We had not long to wait.

Suddenly, clearly audible above the hubbub in the middle distance, rang out a high-pitched, staccato command in Japanese, and the attack was launched. Make no mistake, the Jap was a good soldier as well as a fearless one, and his use of fire and movement commanded our grudging respect.

On they came, accompanied by fire intended to keep our heads down; but our whole line now resounded to volley after volley of fire. Our Bren gunners emptied burst after burst at point blank range and we could see the Japs falling on all sides until they faltered and broke. I immediately gave the order to cease fire, to await the next attack. To my surprise, as our firing died down, there was borne to our ears the chatter of Bren gun fire from above us and, as the Japs continued to fall in front of us, the wireless set buzzed urgently.

In all the noise, it was almost impossible to distinguish the shouting voice of Peter Myers.

'We've got them,' he yelled. 'I can see them all forming up to attack you and I am putting my mortars on to them.'

Sure enough, immediately afterwards came the metallic cough of our own mortars from the ridge and we were treated to an awe-inspiring sight. Bombs were crashing on to the Japanese in a continuous stream, the first arrivals exploding in clods of earth whilst the remainder were still in the air. Three times the Japs formed up and each time we were forewarned by our friends on the hill. Three times they charged and each time their attack petered out in the face of our joint efforts. Finally, the yelling and screaming died down and silence fell on the whole area.

The rest of that day was spent in that peculiar, unreal atmosphere which enshrouds two enemy forces in very close contact. At first, the proximity of the enemy is so disturbing that men stay in their foxholes, their faces turned to the perimeter, ever alert for the sudden attack. When nothing materialises and an hour or two passes by, the first return to reality comes when the stomach begins to cry out for food and it is realised that no one has eaten since just after dawn.

The preparation of food requires movement; water must be fetched and water bottles replenished; cooking requires fire; how are you to burn fires right under the noses of the Japs? Experiments are called for and if, in broad daylight, your cook's enthusiasm betrays your position with a column of blue smoke, then the only reward for his industry will be a cluster of mortar bombs to extinguish all your efforts. It will be realised that our cooking in these difficult circumstances was reduced virtually to nil. For the next three days and nights we existed mainly on our iron rations to sustain us.

After the feeling of close proximity to these Japanese had worn off a little, we took stock of ourselves. As our whole company position was hardly fifty yards wide, an inspection of all posts did not mean a long and arduous journey. However, it did mean constant wading through the waters of the stream. As none of us removed clothing or boots during those next few days, the water turned my boots a horrible blue, mouldy colour. It was clear that during daylight we could do no more than hold our own with our friends above us to give us support and warning of attack; but night would tell a different story.

Sure enough, soon after dark, the enemy started to jitter us on all sides and the night became clamorous with their efforts. That night's jittering followed the familiar pattern and it was a matter of great pride to me, as the shrieks, yells and shots echoed about us, to find that no man fired back.

At intervals, when the hubbub around us died down, we could hear distinctly the sounds of 'C' Company on the hill receiving the same treatment.

With daylight came sanity, but no respite. The enemy, infiltrating in small parties through the thickly-covered ground under the high ridge, had completely surrounded us. They had even occupied the village of Taungdaw itself, only some fifty yards from our trenches.

At about midday, the Japanese moved forward to attack us once again, but were severely dealt with by mortar fire from our friends above us. They finally broke and ran, leaving twenty-five dead on the ground. The tempo of battle was now rising, and for the next forty-eight hours the battle itself raged around our two companies without a break.

At about 1600 hours the Japs opened up on my company from the north with a number of 75 millimetre and infantry guns at point blank range. I have never been so surprised in my life. Somehow my mind had not associated artillery with the 'remnants' of the Arakan Army; but the ear-splitting 'whizz-bang' effect gave me no time to ponder on this extraordinary development. Later evidence showed that the individual Jap soldiers had discarded their personal belongings from their packs and each carried instead a single shell. Such was the dedication of the Japanese military mind.

At this point our own Artillery were unable to fire in our support as the mountain ridge behind us intercepted the fall of the shells – a factor which the Japanese were quick to notice after the first few rounds had gone astray.

Fortunately for us, however, the Jap Artillery was so close to us that most of their shells passed clean through our positions and went sighing and singing down the valley to wreak havoc far outside our battle area. One shell did score a direct hit on the pinnacle of the Poynggi Kyaung but did not explode. Instead, it stuck there at an angle, a bright silver fish-like body, the focus for many an anxious glance during the next two days.

This was not of course the first dud Jap shell which we had seen – there had been several at the Battle of Milaungbya – but it was of great interest. Presumably the Japanese factories were free of sabotage, so the cause of so many duds must have been either faulty workmanship or else the monsoon dampness.

After a while the shelling lifted from us and concentrated on the 'C' Company positions above us. Unhappily they suffered more severely from tree bursts and lost a number of men killed and wounded. The gunfire continued until darkness fell.

When daylight faded, the jittering began again all around us and we realised that sleep was out of the question for the second night in succession. By about 2300 hours it became clear that a really big attack on the hill was imminent from the north and the west. I was sharing a slit trench with Pat Davis who was the only other British Officer with me. We listened carefully as, once again, the yelling and shrieking pierced the night air, rising even above the racket of battle.

CHAPTER FOURTEEN

Lachhiman Gurung, VC

At almost 0100 hours some 200 Japs formed up opposite the platoon position in which Rifleman Lachhiman Gurung lay waiting and the real battle for Taungdaw began.

These Japs belonged to 54 Division from the Arakan and were recognised as shock troops. Their commander had estimated correctly that Rifleman Lachhiman's position was the key to the whole defence of the hill occupied by 'C' Company and they were determined to destroy it.

They started by shouting to the platoon to surrender, show a white flag and lay down their arms. The platoon commander, Jemadar Padamsing Thapa, was a small, neat Gurkha of modest bearing. This quiet little man took up the challenge and shouted back at them every conceivable insult that he could lay his tongue to; we could hardly believe our ears as the words floated down to us.

Whilst this was happening, we ourselves had our hands full coping with a diversionary attack put in with the usual yells and screams; but it was all too obvious to us when the real assault commenced. The shouting on the hill rose to screams; the firing increased to a crescendo and, mixed with it, came the sound of tommy guns and sten guns and the banging of hand grenades.

The forward trench of the platoon was manned by Rifleman Lachhiman with two companions. The enemy commenced by hurling grenades into the position, denoting just how close they were. One of these fell on the lip of Lachhiman's trench and, without hesitation, he seized it and hurled it back. A second fell inside the trench; again, he threw it back. A third grenade landed at his feet. He picked it up and as he was in the act of throwing it, it exploded in his hand, blowing off the fingers, shattering his right arm and severely wounding him in the face, body and right leg. His two companions were also badly wounded and lay helpless in the bottom of the trench.

The official citation of his Victoria Cross reads on:

The enemy, screaming and shouting, now formed up shoulder to. shoulder and attempted to rush the position by sheer weight of numbers. Rifleman Lachhiman Gurung, regardless of his wounds, loaded and fired his rifle with his left hand, maintaining a continuous rate of fire.

Wave after wave of fanatical attacks were thrown in by the enemy, but all were repulsed with heavy casualties. For four hours after being severely wounded Rifleman Lachhiman Gurung remained alone awaiting with perfect calm each attack, meeting it with fire at point blank range from his rifle, determined not to give one inch of ground. Of 87 enemy dead counted in the immediate vicinity of the company's locality, 31 lay in front of this Rifleman's section, the key to the whole position. Had the enemy succeeded in over-running and occupying Rifleman Lachhiman Gurung's trench, the whole of the reverse slope position would have been completely dominated and turned. This Rifleman, by his magnificent example, so inspired his comrades to resist the enemy to the last that, although surrounded and cut off for three days and two nights, they held and smashed every attack. His gallant and extreme devotion to duty in the face of almost overwhelming odds were the main factors in the defeat of the enemy.

One does not presume to add to a graphic citation for bravery. Let it suffice to say that on that night, as the battle raged up and down the hill and around us down below, we were fully aware that if 'C' Company were to be over-run then our position would be at the mercy of the Japanese as soon as daylight came. And now that we know the full story of Rifleman Lachhiman's courage, each of us acknowledges that all our lives were in this boy's hands during those hours of darkness.

Next day brought the aircraft.

As Colonel Walker could not fire on the Japs with artillery, he had requested support from the Royal Air Force.

During the morning of 13th May, whilst we were licking our wounds, we heard suddenly the sound of a solitary aircraft engine and wondered whether this was a trump card produced by the Japs. As we scanned the sky in bewilderment, over came a Hurricane, which circled the area in rather an uncertain fashion and then flew off. Our disappointment was intense for a short while but, a little later, it turned to joy as we heard a hum in the distance, gradually increasing to a roar as a formation of Hurricanes started circling over us in the brilliant blue sky. Suddenly, a single plane detached itself from the group and put its nose down at us in a steep power dive.

It was easy to see the bomb as it left the aircraft and screamed down over our heads. With a shattering roar, the 500-lb bomb hit the village of Taungdaw right in the centre, exactly fifty yards from us, a distance of roughly two and a half times the length of a cricket pitch. We were all thrown about in our foxholes by the tremendous concussion and for a moment I thought that my eardrums had gone.

Another piercing whistle, however, convinced me that they were sound after all as a second bomb followed the first. Down they came, one after another, whilst the village vanished from our sight in crackling sheets of flame and flying pieces of bamboo huts.

Above the roar of the flames came the clatter of cannon fire as the first few planes dived and dived again, raking the village from all sides and then turning their attention to the ridge from which the Japs had been attacking us.

Those pilots were splendid.

During the whole of the next two days they kept up a continuous 'cab-rank' over our heads during daylight and pounded the Japs whenever they saw movement. As a result, the Jap activity was restricted mainly to darkness in our immediate vicinity and it was during the following night that I experienced a nasty personal shock.

In common with everyone else, I had not slept since we had arrived at Taungdaw because of the jitter parties and the attacks. Now I lay down about midnight, determined to snatch some rest. Because of exhaustion, I fell into a deep sleep and did not awake until the first glimmer of dawn. Then habit awoke me. To my horror, the very first thing upon which my eyes focussed was the body of a dead Jap lying some ten yards away, right in the heart of our position. The full implication that he had died so close to my unconscious form was enough to bring out a chill sweat all over me, and I looked quickly around.

My orderly's head was visible over the edge of his slit trench, and when he saw me stirring a wide grin split his face.

'I shot him, Sahib,' he said, and patted his tommygun.

The dead Jap was wearing rubber patrol boots with the divided space for the big toe, rather like a cloven hoof; he had one grenade in his belt, no other equipment, and was grasping a naked bayonet.

We could only presume that he was foraging for food or for information, and we discovered from tracks in the soil that he had entered our position through the stream. I noticed that his chest and arm were already bandaged with blood-soaked rags which in turn had been riddled by the burst of tommy gun bullets.

To appreciate fully what was done to help us in our desperate position, it is necessary now to see what the rest of the battalion were doing to try to save us.

The last ration party had reached us on 11th May along the track and over the col, but the Japs, when they surrounded us, occupied the ground on both sides of the col and by 12th May we were well and truly cut off.

On the 11th, a jeep patrol of five men under a young British officer, Douglas Farnbank, was sent to explore the area south of Yebok for information. They found twenty-five Japs bathing. The sight of such a tempting target was too good to miss and young Douglas immediately attacked them with his small band. Unfortunately, the wily Japanese had concealed machine guns covering their ablutions and our patrol received the worst part of the exchanges.

The officer was badly wounded in both legs by machine gun bursts and without doubt owed his life to a naik (corporal) of the Burma Intelligence Corps who had accompanied the patrol as an interpreter. This brave man, entirely alone, carried him out of range, hid him all day from Jap patrols combing the area, and reported his whereabouts to our troops in Yebok, who eventually brought him in.

Meantime, the Colonel sent 'D' Company to try and relieve pressure upon us by a diversionary attack to the north, behind our opponents. They met large forces of the enemy on 13th May and after killing thirty Japs rejoined the remainder of the battalion in Yebok in the late afternoon.

The dominating ridge that overlooked us in the valley also overlooked Yebok to the east. The enemy on this high ground, seeing troops in Yebok, brought up a heavy mortar and within half an hour was mortaring the village. Unfortunately, the second bomb landed right in the middle of a section of riflemen and killed or wounded six out of nine men. The bombs continued to fall until night came and caused twenty casualties. During the night of 12/13th May, whilst the big attack was taking place on Rifleman Lachhiman's position in 'C' Company on the hill, a party of ten Japs tried to break into the Yebok position and actually pierced the outer perimeter before being killed to a man.

During this night, we in the valley had the unique experience of listening to a fierce battle raging on the hill in front of us, whilst another was joined behind us; we ourselves were coping with jittering. By the morning of 14th May, the position was really serious.

Both 'C' Company and ourselves, as might be expected, were running short of food and ammunition and casualties required evacuation. Unfortunately, amongst others, a British Artillery officer attached to 'C' Company had been shot very badly in the stomach and died eventually after two days of agony. It was clear to the Colonel that the whole battle now hung in the balance.

'A' Company was now brought up to capture the high ground which dominated the col. This was a very difficult task. Mountain ridges, covered in forest provide many obstacles to a smooth advance; the ground itself will always favour the defenders rather than the attackers. As they climbed the ridge to the south and started to work their way along the col the opposition steadily increased. We could distinctly hear the volume of firing rising as the minutes went by.

By about 1100 hours, Mike Tidswell's company had penetrated to within fifty yards of the Japanese positions which were ahead and above. His casualties began to mount and the men were finally pinned to the ground.

Gurkhas, though brave in the extreme, are human. Hot, weary and no doubt exhausted, these men had come to the end of their tether for the time being. When the muscles of your legs refuse to respond to the calls made upon them, when your rifle begins to droop in the grasp of your tired arms – that is the moment of truth. Their comrades were falling on all sides. The survivors went to ground.

I well remember the last words of Colonel Willasey-Wilsey as he said farewell to me at Quetta:

'Denis, the Gurkha is a magnificent soldier, but he must be resolutely led. Do nothing foolish in battle; but you will know in your heart when the time to lead has arrived.'

So it was now with Mike Tidswell. Perhaps the same words were ringing in his ears. It was now the classic situation where the British Officer must accept wounds or even death to reinfuse courage into his men.

It appears that Mike reformed the platoon under cover and then led them in a charge that was immediately successful. The immediate Jap trenches in front were captured, with ten Jap bodies counted. Sad to relate, whilst charging, Mike was hit at once by a sniper. A bullet went through his right arm and into his body, emerging at the top of his spinal cord. Although still able to talk, he was paralysed. They carried him down the slope to Battalion HQ and gently placed him in a jeep ambulance. As the jeep was making its way back to the Advanced Dressing Station, the paralysis reached his lungs and he died. His last words were, 'This is it, Doc.'

Thus we lost one of the finest officers in the battalion. A product of Dulwich College, Mike was always the epitome of charm, courtesy and efficiency. His sense of humour was always present even in the grimmest circumstances and cheered us all at all times. When the news reached us over the wireless my spirit knew true desolation. Later, after the battle, when Peter Myers was gathering Mike's personal belongings together, he held out wordlessly Mike's banjo with which he had entertained us at Kohima and I broke down for the first time in all those dreadful months.

When Mike fell to the sniper's bullet his orderly, consumed by grief and rage, dashed forward without thought for his own safety and shot the Jap out of a tree; he finished him off as he lay on the ground.

Despite some local success, the company was still as a whole unable to reach their objective and they were ordered to consolidate the position won, which was some 200 yards south of the col.

By evening a very gloomy atmosphere prevailed at Battalion HQ. Five of 'C' Company wounded had already died of their wounds and many more were likely to succumb. The strain was telling on all concerned; to add to the general discomfort it had started to rain heavily during the evening.

Colonel Walker now made his final plan.

Scotty Gilmore had taken over command of 'A' Company when Mike was hit. The Colonel asked him over the wireless whether he considered that he could cope. Scotty's reply was succinct and immortal:

'I sure can, Colonel. You send me the ammunition and I'll finish the job.' Such was the spirit that was bred by those days of companionship and hardship under fire. Walter Walker promoted Scotty to Major over the wireless, on the spot. Thus it was that our charming American could claim perhaps to be the only 'British Officer' to be promoted in the field.

Walter Walker's plan was for 'D' Company to assault the ridge at its highest point and then swing down it to the col. They set out at 0800 hours next day in a tense atmosphere and slowly climbed up and up. By 1000 hours they had reached the high summit and started to attack the col itself. We could hear firing but not in the degree to which we had become accustomed. Our troops found comparatively few Japanese in their positions and despatched them without delay.

Meanwhile, we in our positions had been holding off the Japs around us and as their pressure weakened we patrolled into the village of Taungdaw which by this time was unrecognisable as a village; shattered bamboo huts, ankle deep in ashes; trees splintered and uprooted; gardens ploughed by bomb craters. Japanese bodies lay everywhere in grotesque positions and the sickly-sweet smell of death tainted the air on all sides.

It was on this day that we captured our first Japanese prisoner.

We found him squatting in a slit trench, cackling with laughter. I was convinced that he was suffering from shell-shock and I bent over him to search his pockets for documents. The stale fumes of rice wine rose in a stench and struck me full in the face. He was blind drunk. In the corner of the trench was a vast jar – empty.

On the morning of 15th May events moved swiftly to a happy ending.

We were not attacked ourselves but we could hear the firing up in the direction of the col. We could not trace the course of events but it all meant that the battalion was still trying to succour us. It was very heartening to our deafened ears, tired bodies and numbed minds. We still expected another Jap attack and were manning our trenches and watching carefully to the north from whence we thought it would come. Ammunition was low, food scarce and we reckoned that even now just one more heavy attack would probably use up all our reserves. After that the bayonet and kukri would be our last means of defence. I gave orders to hold fire until the Japs would be ten or fifteen yards away. With strained faces we waited, on the alert.

Suddenly we saw figures running towards us and we crouched, tense and ready. I repeated my order to hold fire.

As the figures drew closer and closer, they were shouting and gesticulating wildly. They were not wearing Japanese helmets; they were wearing turbans. These were not Japs, they were Sikhs. They were the advanceguard of the 1/11th Sikhs, our old friends from Kohima days.

As they rushed forward, our men climbed wearily from their trenches and rushed to meet them with cheers. With much hugging and backslapping, the two regiments mingled, forging still another link in that mysterious bond that united us all.

Amongst the advancing figures I recognised the figure of their company commander who was known personally to me. As I advanced to meet him I saw that he had tears in his eyes. He told me that only a few moments before, a young Sikh officer, who was his second-in-command, had been shot dead by a Jap sniper. I had myself met this youngster several weeks previously when he had returned from his honeymoon in India. Like his British company commander I felt quite overcome by his untimely and tragic death. A picture of his heartbroken young bride flashed across my mind, and in that instant I felt very, very old.

A few minutes after the Sikhs had broken through to us from the north, we heard the sounds of shouting and cheering breaking out on our eastern perimeter as the stocky, jaunty figures of our own Gurkhas from 'D' Company came pouring into our positions after driving the Japs off the ridge. Close behind them came a jeep, bumping over the rough ground. It halted, and out stepped Colonel Walker and Geoffrey Bull.

The enthusiasm was terrific.

Men from both companies mingled everywhere in groups, laughing and chattering and relating their own particular adventures to anyone who cared to listen.

The men of my company were very amused because our relief column arrived with most of the men wearing handkerchiefs over their noses because of the smell of the bloated and fly-ridden Japanese corpses lying around us. We had become so accustomed to the smell that we noticed nothing unusual about it until we saw the faces of our saviours.

After the mutual congratulations were over, the Colonel ordered us to join Battalion HQ without delay. It was a very weary but proud company that marched out and back up the ridge, with many a backward glance at that valley which, in four days, had been transformed from a picture of peace and serenity to a besmirched and shattered landscape, over which the first vultures were already circling.

CHAPTER FIFTEEN

Nyaungkashe

The battle of Taungdaw brought to an end my personal involvement in the fighting in Burma. A week or so after the battle I was evacuated from the battle zone suffering from the effects of battle exhaustion; the remainder of my time with the regiment was devoted to training recruits and passing on the experience gained on active service.

I had heard of the phrase 'battle exhaustion' but had never ever considered myself to be a candidate for this rather all-embracing diagnosis. The ability of the human being to stand up to mental and physical strain is really surprising. However, there comes a time when the combined and continuous strains bring an individual to the final limits of endurance. It is not a question of courage or lack of courage. The constant physical exertion that steadily drains the limbs of response, the lack of sleep night after night, all combine to dull the mind and rob it of the alertness and ability to react which are essential qualities to survival in the case of any soldier in action. To my chagrin I began to suffer from unaccountable lapses of memory. Intensive training had been instigated by our new CO, Colonel Walker having left us after the battle on promotion to higher echelons.

Instead of being able to concentrate on the intricacies of training programmes and locations, my mind continued to dwell on and recall the boom of artillery and the crash of bursting shells, the stutter of machine guns, the roar of exploding grenades and the crackle of rifle and tommy gun fire. Over and over again, the faces of the wounded and dying appeared before me until I was no longer living in the present but in the immediate past. The sudden transition from the battlefield to such training in such a short time was too quick. I could neither concentrate nor conform. My reserves of energy had vanished. Somewhere behind me, on the banks of the Irrawaddy, in the shattered remains of Milaungbya, or by the forested slopes of Taungdaw, I seemed to have left my true self; I had now become an empty shell.

As I tried to conceal my feelings from my brother officers and from the men of my company, I suffered a mental withdrawal from those around me. The inability to think clearly and the necessity to appear normal finally brought my faculties to a stand-still and the doctor intervened.

With hindsight it is easy to see the remedy – withdrawal from combat, rest, regular meals and sleep; above all, the sleep which we all craved. One day, as if participating in a dream, I found myself being shepherded by the kindly doctor and an anxious CO to our jeep ambulance on the first leg of my flight out of Burma to India. My feelings were a strange mixture of total mental relief and remorse at leaving behind my companions-in-arms who might yet have to face still more hardships and battle. Above all, I kept wondering what my company would do without me. It is strange that we so often consider ourselves to be indispensable even when brought low by misfortune. In the interim weeks I was granted a fresh experience as I passed through the wards of the advanced and then the base hospitals. There, I saw firsthand what the horrors of war had done to the minds of dozens of other casualties, particularly British troops; men whose previous backgrounds of office desk or factory workbench, school classroom or representative's daily round had not prepared them for their ordeal of killing and maiming, blood and sudden death under the pitiless Burma sun. I was filled with pity as I saw men whose incoherent mumblings and vacant stares betrayed the fact that their minds had been destroyed by the hardships and horrors of the Burma Campaign.

Rest and treatment brought me back from the edge of the same abyss. In due course I walked out of the hospital at Comilla in the company of a captain from the South Lancashire Regiment. A few weeks earlier, this officer had been brought in, a shivering, trembling case of shellshock, his head spasmodically jerking on his shoulders so that it was totally impossible for me to insert a lighted cigarette into his mouth. We shook hands like civilised people as we parted, two individuals restored to sanity.

Calcutta was my first port of call whilst in transit. There I experienced once again the delights of civilised surroundings; fresh linen sheets, soft beds, first class food served up on tablecloths amidst silver cutlery and linen napkins; occasionally, the delights of feminine company and even the dimly remembered pleasure of the dance floor. I well remember that the cinemas in Calcutta were air-conditioned and the pleasure of luxuriating in their cool, dark interiors almost outweighed other more sophisticated delights after the rigours of Burma.

In due course I left the fleshpots behind me and boarded the train for my long journey, lasting some four or five days, across India; back up to those arid hills of Baluchistan, peopled by the hook-nosed, fierce-visaged Pathans. Finally, I arrived at the portals of the training centre and entered once again the world of the white-washed guardroom, immaculate uniforms, staccato commands and the rattle and crash of drill movements performed under the eagle eyes and high-pitched scream of the instructors. I was home.

Once more I fitted into the pattern of this familiar world whilst a corner of my mind kept reverting to the battalion. Were they all still by the Irrawaddy or had they reached Rangoon – that goal for which we had all striven? Had they been in action again and had they survived? Was 'B' Company intact? Suddenly, out of the blue, the news broke. It came in the shape of a long letter from Tony Brand Crombie who was in hospital, wounded. It was worse than I had expected. In fact, disaster had struck.

I read that 'B' Company had been partially destroyed.

By 19th June 1945 the 7th Indian Division had been moved from the Irrawaddy to the line of the Sittang River, the border between Burma and Siam. The orders were to prevent the remnants of the Japanese army from breaking out and escaping across the border.

The 4/8th were concentrated in the region of a village named Nyaungkashe, some two miles from the Sittang Bridge position; the bridge which had been blown up by our retreating forces in 1942 and which is known so well to the survivors of that retreat.

The monsoon had broken and at this time the conditions for our battalion in this area were appalling. The countryside was flat with no cover; it was interspersed with villages or hamlets a mile or two apart, dense little areas of trees and houses, waterlogged and muddy. In between the villages was a wilderness of water and mud, paddy and coarse kiang grass, leeches, mosquitoes, rats and Japanese. It was here that the battalion became involved in its last battle on Burmese soil, a battle which surpassed in severity any that had gone before and brought in its train severe casualties.It even warranted a paragraph in the English Press under the headline: 'The Battle of the Sittang Bends'.

Owing to the terrain and the conditions, companies and platoons were spread around in isolated locations with attendant difficulties in supplying them with food, fresh water and ammunition. At one stage, 'B' Company, aided in the latter stages by 'A' Company, less one platoon, attacked a small village over flooded paddyfields, the water reaching the men's knees, and in part their waists. After bitter fighting, the village was captured but, owing to its filthy condition and the fact that it was waterlogged, it was decided not to occupy it. In this engagement, Rifleman Manbir Ale exhibited extreme gallantry. Unable to fire his Bren gun from the lying position owing to the state of the ground, Manbir stood up and, firing from the hip, covered his section attack on a Japanese machine gun position in a bunker. His right hand and lower arm were at once smashed by bullets from the bunker. Nevertheless, this gallant soldier, supporting his gun on his shattered arm, carried on firing until he fell, mortally wounded. He was later awarded a posthumous Mention in Despatches.

At another stage, the battalion came under the most concentrated shellfire yet seen in that theatre of war. On the night of 5/6th July, in the space of twenty minutes, no less than 145 shells from large and small guns from both sides of the Sittang fell into the battalion headquarter area. The Regimental Aid Post, already full of wounded, received a direct hit. The Adjutant, Captain Quentin Kennedy and others were killed or received further wounds. The Medical Officer, Captain I.A. Dalton, IAMC, and Captain Tony Brand Crombie were also wounded.

'B' Company were in position in a wooded garden one mile to the west of Nyaungkashe, together with three 25 pounder guns, all isolated from the battalion. In turn, one of their platoons – No 4 Platoon, under the command of Jemadar Manbahadur Gurung –

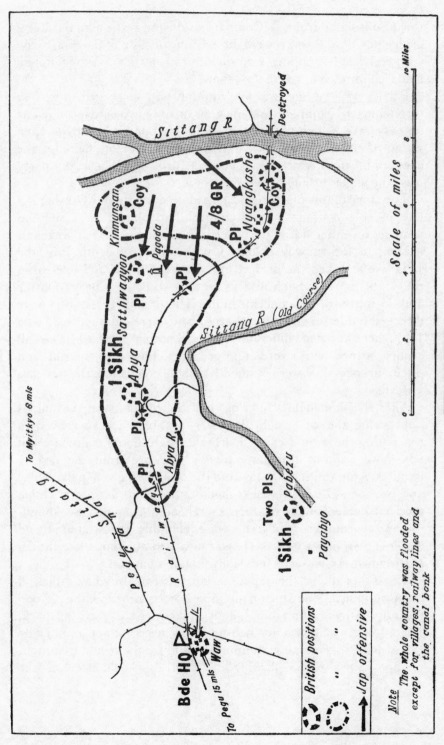

SITTANG BEND
Night, 3rd-4th July, 1945

was also isolated from 'B' Company and were at the actual railway bridge position. Rations were received by air drop, but owing to the very restricted dropping zone in the railway station area, many loads fell into the hands of the Japanese.

Parties with rations and ammunition had succeeded in getting through to 'B' Company and the guns on only two occasions. It was no easy task, which involved crossing five hundred yards of open water, overlooked from the railway embankment, held by the enemy and from which heavy fire was brought to bear. No party was able to get through to No 4 Platoon.

The story of this platoon and Jemadar Manbahadur Gurung is a tale of epic courage and discipline. The platoon was sited in trenches on either side of the railway line on top of the embankment leading to the railway bridge. On the night of 3/4th July, the Japanese attacked the bridge, first from the north and later from the south as well. Such attacks were preceded by heavy mortar and 75 mm artillery concentrations. The first three assaults were direct shoulder-to-shoulder charges and were all repulsed. The Japs then adopted different tactics, coming forward in small groups, armed with swords and grenades. Owing to the rain and pitch darkness they were frequently able to creep up to the trenches unseen.

After the first night's fighting, half the platoon were casualties but during the next night Jemadar Manbahadur succeeded in evacuating the serious cases. During daylight hours the men could not move without bringing down sniper fire from the nearby hamlets. Ammunition was low and the order was given to use Kukri and bayonet. During the next night Lance-Naik Sarsaram Thapa received a severe sword cut on the forehead during a series of hand-to-hand encounters whilst he was defending the wounded and helpless men in his trench. He was awarded an Immediate Indian Distinguished Conduct Medal for this gallant action.

The same night, the Japanese launched an infantry attack of about fifty men, following an intensive bombardment of the platoon position. After a short but bloody encounter the Japs fell back, leaving twenty-five bodies behind. This fierce attack practically exhausted the remaining ammunition and for the rest of that night to cope with alternate shelling and infiltration cold steel was the only available reply. The ordeal of this platoon was shared by one section of medium machine guns of the 13th Frontier Force Rifles Medium Machine Gun Battalion who had also been with us at Milaungbya. They manned their guns until both were knocked out by shellfire. Their casualties were as heavy as our own.

Four separate attempts were made by day and by night to succour this platoon with ammunition and reinforcements but all were forced back by heavy and accurate fire.

On the night of 5th July the usual attacks were put in and repulsed by the defenders. At midnight the attackers finally withdrew and there followed a really tremendous bombardment. Every trench was knocked to pieces and the surviving Gurkhas were forced out on to the railway line. After three days and nights of continuous fighting without even a brew of tea for comfort, these men appeared to be indifferent to their fate, being in a strange mental and physical state which Jemadar Manbahadur later described as akin to drunkenness.

The Japanese lost no time in following up their success; the five leading Japs were bayonetted and the remaining wavered and fell back. However, determined to make an end of the platoon's resistance, the enemy lined up once again with all his remaining strength and advanced to the embankment. At this point, Manbahadur realised that he and his platoon had done everything in their power to hold the position and he ordered the survivors to withdraw on 'B' Company. Of a total of approximately thirty men, he had now only seven left, five of whom were wounded.

The story of one section of Manbahadur's platoon is in keeping with the whole epic. This section was at the north-west end of the bridge and had been isolated from the rest of the platoon since the first attack. Of seven men in the section, three were killed and two captured; one, badly wounded, was reported missing whilst the seventh, left the sole occupant, escaped from the position and, eluding the Japanese, finally rejoined the forward company of the 1/11th Sikhs several days later. One of them, already wounded in the leg, had been used by the Japanese for light machine gun target practice; he bit through his bonds and, with both legs shattered, dragged himself through the water of the paddyfields for several miles.

Jemadar Manbahadur Gurung, for supreme devotion to duty, outstanding personal gallantry and his defence of the position to the last round and all but the last man, was awarded an Immediate Military Cross.

By mid-day on 6th July, the battle had raged for sixty-five hours. At this stage, orders were received for the whole battalion to fight its way out to the HQ of the 1/11th Sikhs. This fine battalion had made several attempts to clear the way down the railway line but on each, in spite of superb gallantry and determination, had been repulsed.

The story of the battalion withdrawal was again in keeping with that of the battle of Nyaungkashe. 'B' Company, with the Royal Artillery personnel and the medium machine gun section, withdrew into Nyaungkashe, having destroyed their reserve ammunition and rendered the three 25 pounder guns useless. I learned later that my own remaining personal belongings which had been left behind when I went into hospital were also destroyed. At 2115 hours the battalion commenced withdrawal but, unfortunately, the 89 Indian Infantry Brigade plan to extricate the survivors miscarried. Owing to the pitch darkness of a monsoon night and the widely separated lines of platoon groups, contact with the 4/8th, in the shape of guides and a rearguard, was never effected.

In a terrain devoid of landmarks, in pitch darkness and heavy rain, the withdrawal was completed after a night march. Wading, often nearly swimming, through the chaungs, squelching through leech-infested grass and plough, the march was accomplished without the loss of a single man. The efforts of the stretcher-bearers, carrying sick and wounded in these truly appalling conditions, were nothing short of miraculous.

For the battalion, the events of this night indeed also bordered on the miraculous. Firstly, there was no shelling; the Japanese were busy shelling the railway line and station at Abya, some five miles to the north-west. Secondly, no enemy were encountered on the ground, although those sent out from other units to assist the withdrawal had seen numbers of them in the area.

When I read the letter describing these events, I was stunned as the story unfolded. In my mind's eye I could see my 'B' Company in their isolation amongst the flooded paddyfields. Jemadar Manbahadur's No 4 Platoon was the same platoon upon whom our own shells had fallen at Milaungbya, during our first battle. Now only a handful of these men were still alive. Amongst the dead was my orderly, Dilbahadur.

I was also deeply saddened to learn that Quentin Kennedy was listed amongst those killed in action. To have been wounded one day and then killed whilst lying in the apparent safety of the Regimental Aid Post somehow emphasised the horror of the whole story. Quentin was a great personal friend of Mike Tidswell whose death at Taungdaw had already affected me deeply.

It is difficult to explain the bond that united us all in a Gurkha infantry battalion. To describe us all as a family would offend the sceptic of to-day, but like a family we were in our relationship with each other and with the men. We were truly 'brother' officers and we regarded the men with affection and admiration as we would our children. I felt sick at the slaughter of No 4 Platoon and it was a very long time indeed before I was able to erase a feeling of guilt at having been missing at their greatest time of need.

The battle of Nyaungkashe signalled the end of the Burma Campaign for the 4/8th Gurkha Rifles, although the battalion was later engaged in patrolling and guard duties at bridges and road junctions to prevent the Japanese break-out to the east. Within a month, the Atom Bomb had been dropped on Japan and the Japanese had subsequently surrendered unconditionally.

The exotic and almost unpronounceable names of Milaungbya, Taungdaw and Nyaungkashe joined such names as Ngakydauk, 'Admin Box', Buthidaung, Imphal and Ukhrul to gain a worthy place amongst the honours won by the 8th Gurkha Rifles in former wars.

Such honours are not won without sacrifice and the cost to the 4/8th alone during the Camapign tells its own story:.

Killed

British and Gurkha Officers	13
Gurkha Other ranks	124

Died of Wounds

British and Gurkha Officers   2
Gurkha Other Ranks   28

Missing Presumed Dead

Gurkha Other Ranks   11
Non-Combatants   1

Wounded

British and Gurkha Officers   20
Gurkha Other Ranks   355

EPILOGUE

At last the war in Burma was over and the next destination of the 4/8th turned out to be Siam. In these new surroundings in Bangkok the battalion was engaged in guard duties which occupied a great deal of time. In contrast, this westernised and sophisticated city had many attractions to offer to officers and men alike. In December orders were received for a further move and the battalion set sail for Malaya where it stayed for some six months engaged in internal security duties.

It is interesting to note that the 7th Indian Division, to which we belonged, were the first Allied troops to enter enemy-occupied territory in south-east Asia. It disarmed and concentrated 113,000 Japanese; some 20,000 United Kingdon and Australian ex-prisoners of war were evacuated, and the division succoured no less than 20,000 coolies who had been conscripted for labour on the notorious Moulmein railway, known as the Railway of Death and which figured in the post-war film *Bridge over the River Kwai*.

On 13th June 1945, after serving with the 7th Indian Division for four and a half years, the battalion took leave of the division and was ordered to embark at Singapore for Java. Three days later, the ship reached its destination and the battalion was posted to the 37th Indian Infantry Brigade which was guarding the Batavia area.

The situation in Java at this time was chaotic. The interior was in the hands of Indonesians whose mode of anarchical government did not commend itself to the Allied Governments. Dutch and Eurasian women and children accommodated in Japanese concentration camps, whose homes were now in Indonesian hands, had to be rescued. Lawless gangs and bands of Japanese soldiers who had not surrendered had to be rounded up. Once more the battalion was called upon to play its part under circumstances of which it has been said: 'The chaotic must be regarded as normal'.

During these operations, designed to restore law and order, the battalion suffered the loss of the final casualties of the Second World War, including the death of Subadar Kharakbahadur Gurung in fierce hand-to-hand fighting in the vicinity of Bekassi. This splendid officer was the one who had returned to our 'B' Company position at Milaungbya, in Burma, bearing the head of the Japanese scout, all those months previously.

In due course the last move took place when the battalion moved to Batavia to take over the guarding of the docks. After five weeks in this hot and dirty neighbourhood all ranks were delighted to embark on TS *Talma* for Malaya which was reached at Port Swettenham on 21st November 1946. In pleasant surroundings, near Kuala Lumpur, the battalion's term of active service in the Second World War came to an end. It had fought in mountain and valley, in jungle and plain; it had crossed rivers and swamps, leaving behind an ever increasing toll of dead and carrying with it the surviving wounded and the stricken sick. Of the total casualty list of the 8th Gurkha Rifles during this war, amounting to 1,942 including 584 dead, the casualties of the 4/8th Battalion constituted a large proportion.

The award of medals for acts of gallantry is regarded in some quarters as archaic or, at least, unfair to those whose courage in some dirty corner of a battlefield has gone unnoticed or unsung. However, to complete the record it should be recorded that the following awards were received by the officers and men of the 4/8th:

Victoria Cross	1
Distinguished Service Order	1
Indian Order of Merit	2
Military Cross	12
Bar to Military Cross	1
Indian Distinguished Service Medal	12
Military Medal	22
Mention in Despatches	39
Certificate of Gallantry	6

The end of the war brought drastic changes in its wake.

Rifleman Lachhiman Gurung, vc, spent a considerable time in

hospital recovering from his severe wounds. He subsequently returned to the Regimental Training Centre and was promoted to havildar. He was employed as mess havildar in the Officers' Mess but finally went on pension and returned to Nepal. I had the great pleasure of meeting him again many years after the war when, in 1974, he was included in a party of ex-Indian Army VCs who visited London and attended a cocktail party given by the India High Commissioner.

It was inevitable that the officers of the battalion should part and go their separate ways as the majority of us were Emergency Commissioned Officers, in 'for the duration of hostilities'. To the best of my recollection, only three were Regular officers.

Undoubtedly the officer whose career reached the pinnacle of success in later years was Colonel (later General Sir) Walter Walker. It is impossible to convey in a few lines the compass of this illustrious career. Let it suffice to record that he was awarded the DSO in Burma for his outstanding services, a Bar to the DSO in 1953 when commanding his battalion against the Communist terrorists in Malaya and a second Bar when he was Director of Borneo Operations during that very difficult campaign. Other honours include the CBE during the Malayan Emergency in 1959 and the KCB in 1968. Amongst the various appointments held by this fine soldier were: GOC Northern Command, England; Deputy Chief of Staff in charge of Plans, Operations and Intelligence, HQ Allied Forces Central Europe; in 1969 he was appointed NATO Commander-in-Chief Allied Forces Northern Europe, where he served until 1972 when he retired from the Army after forty years service.

Peter Myers stayed on in the Army after the war and attained the rank of brigadier after serving with distinction in Malaya and Borneo.

Of the remainder, over the years I managed to keep in touch with quite a few and it is interesting to note the diverse careers which they followed in peacetime. Peter Wickham joined the BBC Overseas Staff; Tony Brand Crombie became an executive in the engineering world. Pat Davis took a degree in English Literature at Oxford and subsequently produced a book entitled *A Child at Arms* which was awarded a prize for a first publication by a new author.

'Doc' Dalton went into private medical practice in London; Bob Findlay, whose family were 'in' teak in Burma, lives in a castle by Loch Lomond in Scotland; Peter Dickinson is now a lieutenant-colonel in the Army Educational Corps. Scott Gilmore returned to America where he became an executive in the family publishing house. Brian Irving lives outside Reading and is a leading light in the hockey world.

Sally and I met up again in India and were married in Kashmir, returning to England in 1946. Our daughter, Margaret, was born in 1947. Returning to the Insurance world which I had left at the age of twenty-three, I continued my career in London until retirement in 1974. Having settled in Wales, I then undertook a second career in Civil Defence as Deputy County Emergency Planning Officer for the County of Dyfed; I retired for the second time after the tragic death of my wife in 1978. I then emigrated to South Africa where Margaret had already settled some years previously. In South Africa I met again a very old friend of the family since 1945 – Mary MacHorton – who had arrived there several years previously. We were married in 1980. I am glad to say that we are continuing to live 'happily ever after'.

Appendix I

ORDER OF THE DAY

BY

LT.-COL. W.C. WALKER,
COMMANDING 4/8th GURKHA RIFLES.

20 DECEMBER 1944

The Battalion is once again about to proceed on active operations against the Japanese.

Most of us have had leave and most of us have undergone intensive training to fit ourselves for active service.

The results of our training have been excellent, and if we all not only remember what we have learned but put it into practice against the Japanese, we shall annihilate him on every occasion we fight him in battle.

We have had to face difficulties but all ranks have never given up trying, never lost faith and never forgotten the cause which has brought us together in this Battalion. And the result – the joint result – of it all is a real live regiment, with a morale and soul of its own.

Those of you who have not fought against the Japanese before have no knowledge as to what your real strength or weaknesses may be. Some of you, hitherto undistinguished, will come into your own and cover yourselves with glory. Only war itself can discover the qualities which count in war. But I am definitely confident that the supreme Gurkha virtue – the virtue of holding on, and holding on, and holding on, until our task is accomplished – will not be found wanting in a single one of you.

The fighting in front of us will be tough and we shall have to exert every ounce of our strength. But we shall defeat the enemy just as we have defeated him before, and just as other Gurkha battalions have defeated not only the Japanese but the Germans also.

The reputation of Gurkhas as fighting men is unsurpassed. You are known throughout the world as the best fighters of any army, and the enemy respects you and fears you. The Gurkha brigade has already received 7 VCs, the highest award that can be won for gallantry. We ourselves have received 2 IOMs, 3 MCs, 3 IDSMs, 6 MMs and 1 Gallantry Certificate. All these have been Immediate Awards. There are more awards to come as a result of our fighting in the Arakan and Imphal area. As yet no battalion of the 8th Gurkhas has received a VC – let us be the first Battalion to achieve this signal honour.

I know we shall kill and utterly destroy the Japanese whenever and wherever we meet him. As Commandant of this Battalion I pin my faith in you. You have character: you have grit and guts; you have supreme courage; you have high morale; you have discipline; you have pride in your race; and now that you have confidence as a result of our recent training, you are all going to be an everlasting credit to the cause which roused the manhood of Nepal and the land which gave you birth.

Appendix II

Typed copy of pencilled message received from
Lt. Col. Walker after the battle of
Milaungbya in Burma. March 1945.

4 Mar. 45.

My Dear Denis,

My very heartiest congratulations on your magnificent display of guts and determination yesterday. You, B Coy. and the Mtr. Sec. under your command, more than upheld the motto of the regiment, and our own Bn. motto.

I am exceedingly sorry that 3 men were killed and 11 wounded. The enemy paid a very heavy price for their abortive attempt to drive you off a feature which was vital to the task given to me – namely, to deny to the enemy the line of the MYAUNG CHAUNG.

As I told you last night over the 'phone, I received the following personal message from the Bde. Commander.

'Please convey to all ranks the appreciation of both the CHAMPION Commander and myself on your successful battle to-day. Well done.'

The credit is *entirely* yours. I have claimed the following casualties.

Killed by Sigs. line party and escort –	10
Killed by MMGs. –	5
Killed by your Coy. and lying WEST of your position last night –	20
Inside your perimeter –	2
Lying 300 yds. outside C. Coy's perimeter –	2
	39

The actual bag must have been many more than this, *excluding wounded.*

I have reported that the strength of the enemy was between 300 and 500.

Please give me as early as possible 'write-ups' including your highly successful raid the other night.

Your own efforts will not go unrewarded.

I am exceedingly proud of you and your Company – please tell them so.

I hope you will be able to produce a number of identifications. The General is particularly anxious that we should produce as many as possible, because he believes that the attack must have been launched by a new battalion, as the original battalion opposing us has already been very badly mauled, and could hardly have produced 300-500 men for such a determined attack.

Your immediate task now is:

1. To secure the ridge to your front.
2. To consolidate the whole position.
3. To hold on to this position *at all costs*.
4. To patrol vigorously to LEGAN and subsequently to PYINGYAUNG.
5. Lastly, to give me more identifications!! Please *comb* the area around you, *including YWATHIT*. The latter place and the environs might well produce several bodies.

I shall come out to you this morning, and we will discuss MMG allotment, etc.

In the meantime let me say – Thank you.

> Yours,
> Walter Walker (sgd.)

P.S.

Make sure, won't you, that your little men keep their precious heads, bless them, below the sky line. No movement on forward slopes – they must patrol in groups of NOT more than 3, move stealthily by bounds – i.e.

DOWN – CRAWL – OBSERVE – LOOK AND LISTEN.

INDEX

INDEX